BEING WITH AND SAYING GOODBYE

BEING WITH AND SAYING GOODBYE

Cultivating Therapeutic Attitude in Professional Practice

Andrew West

KARNAC

First published in 2016 by
Karnac Books Ltd
118 Finchley Road
London NW3 5HT

British Library Cataloguing in Publication Data

A C.I.P. for this book is available from the British Library

ISBN-13: 978-1-78220-336-0

Typeset by V Publishing Solutions Pvt Ltd., Chennai, India

Printed in Great Britain

www.karnacbooks.com

CONTENTS

ACKNOWLEDGEMENTS

From my earliest moments I have been fortunate in having encountered remarkable, loving, astute, patient, provocative, amusing, frightening, inspiring, infuriating, consoling, like-minded, and other-minded people. I should take this opportunity to thank them all. Convention dictates, however, that I select some for particular mention with an eye to the current context. Interview panels, for example, that have seen behind whatever façade the circumstances provoked, and offered me the opportunity to study and then work in medicine, psychiatry, and child and adolescent psychiatry. It would be disingenuous to say that "my patients have taught me everything"—they haven't, but I still don't understand why anyone with reason to distrust adults should place so much trust in me. The same goes for their parents. Without their unwitting collaboration this book could not have been written. Dr. Steve McKeown started me off on psychotherapy, Dr. Fred Hirst was a blast of humanity at a crucial time, Dr. Gillian Forrest taught me clinical rigour and Dr. Pieter van Boxel taught me clinical humour. Friends, family, and colleagues have shaped me in countless ways that I do not fully understand. I thank Cathy Burges and Richard Rogers for their helpful comments on early drafts of the first and final chapters, respectively, and Karey Taylor for her constructive reading of the whole at a later stage. Finally, but not least, I thank Karnac Books for their early interest and subsequent patience.

Oxford, 2015

ABOUT THE AUTHOR

Andrew West grew up in a large family in which idealism, medicine, the sciences, and teaching dominated. With a First in Natural Sciences from Cambridge University he went on to study Medicine in Leeds and Oxford. He has wide interests and therapeutic experience including group and family systemic therapies and works as a child and adolescent psychiatrist in the National Health Service. For the last twenty-five years he has worked part-time in order to share in raising his children.

INTRODUCTION

Written with some urgency, this book describes an attitude that I believe to be necessary for the promotion of professionalism generally, and essential to the ethical practice of child and adolescent mental health work. I call it "attitude" rather than "model" because it seems to me that, once the attitude is struck, the model flows naturally and without further instruction and, what is more, I believe it to be relevant whatever therapeutic model one is working in. I particularly choose not to call it a therapy because there are now far too many therapies. They have become competitive commodities many of which prove, predictably enough, to be short-lived. In contrast, the work is ancient and perpetual.

The urgency of my writing comes from the current proliferation and bedding-in of structures, values, and practices that I consider to be largely incompatible with this therapeutic attitude.

We have all been children and much of what I describe will be recognisable from general experience. This book may therefore be of interest to the general public, but it is directed chiefly towards those who provide professional and developmental services to children and adolescents. Its relevance should stretch beyond child and adolescent psychiatry, which is simply my own professional discipline, through all work in child and adolescent mental health, teaching and social care, and possibly into general and paediatric medical practice.

This is not an authoritative book. It describes my own personal experience and view and the reader must take responsibility for whatever conclusions they draw from reading it. It is not a textbook. It does not attempt to describe the nature and breadth of child and adolescent mental health. It will not methodically cover diagnostic categories, developmental stages, or investigative approaches. It will refer to therapeutic modalities for the purpose of illustration, but its focus is on how we influence, and therefore need to take responsibility for, those *other* things that take place in the relational context whilst the business of assessment, diagnosis, and treatment is taking place: what happens *between the lines*.

What happens between the lines, whilst crucially important, is not routinely taught. It is not embodied in national guidelines or the instructions given to the commissioners of health or education services largely because it cannot easily be apprehended, described, or measured using the methods and terminology currently in vogue. It is something of a ghost in the machine. I am fairly confident that it plays a powerful part in determining the efficacy of our interventions. Correspondingly, failure to attend to it will result in therapeutic inefficiency and raise the risk of un-therapeutic practice and the shameful travesties of care that we read about. Because clinicians are becoming less free to practice according to professionally informed instinct, and because it is never mentioned in the service specifications of the machine, this ghost is at risk of extinction.

Clinical work is a very personal activity. One of the features of our accelerated, materially motivated and financially constrained times is a drive to make these activities less personal. Despite research, personal experience, and common sense, all of which affirm the importance of personal qualities in the therapist, therapies are increasingly manualised in an apparent attempt to eradicate this personal contribution. This is, in my view, neither in the wider interests of humanity, nor in the interests of the individual.

Beyond the health services, the integrity and reputation of individual professionalism as a whole appears to be under similar threat. It is my hope that any expression of what individual professionalism can look like in a specific context could help to prevent its more widespread loss.

My own experience is of the practice of child and adolescent psychiatry in a publicly funded service. I therefore make my argument in that arena. But it is a fitting arena for another reason: the argument is most powerful in relation to mental health where subjective experience is, or should be, the intended product. It is also at its most poignant when the healthy development of a child is at stake.

If what I have to say proves to be comprehensible, it would be a useful exercise to extend "patient" and "clinician" to, respectively, any vulnerable person in need of a service and the appropriately skilled professional with an ongoing duty of care. I am trying to define the relatively indefinable—the ghost or the space, as I have said, between things that have already been amply defined. Given its intangibility and subjectivity I attempt to apprehend it through multiple approaches. Metaphor, case vignette, repetition, hyperbole, and reason will be my sheepdogs as I corral the elusive ideas of importance.

What I have to say has been influenced directly and indirectly by a wide range of writing and practice that has emerged over the years thanks to the efforts and brilliance of therapists and theoreticians of differing persuasions. I have an eclectic interest and have not pursued any one of these approaches to the exclusion of the others. I like ideas that are graspable, useful, and can be talked about in relatively normal language. Much of the vocabulary of the psychotherapies has a poetic appeal, evoking, perhaps, more than they intended. I hope that purists will not be too offended by what may appear to them as something of a pick-and-mix approach. I hope that the product demonstrates hybrid vigour.

I have changed the names and obscured the identities of patients, altering their stories to do so. In research terms this could be seen as the manipulation of data. For case histories to be ethical they have to be fictionalised, and yet they must not lie. Somehow the truth must be conveyed, without the truth being conveyed. Art and science believe themselves to influence in such different ways. I declare myself to be a scientist by training, but predominantly an artist by practice and you will detect, if you read further, my frustration at the extent to which art is disregarded as evidence.

Related to this is my concern at the difficulty that certain voices seem to encounter in being heard. How might diffidence hold sway, for example? It is my job to hear and uphold the child's voice and help it to find direction and expression. I therefore try to give my own resolute uncertainties the same species of encouragement. Whether it is my patients' views or my own that require a firm voice to speak on their behalf, it falls to me to speak as firmly as I can, even if what I want to get across is the fact that we should be more diffident.

Medical training and practice offer an extraordinary range of experience. They carry one across boundaries and taboos on a regular basis, frequently without acknowledging the fact. They also instil, perhaps at the risk of dogmatic or narrow-minded grandiosity, a deep-seated eclecticism and professionalism that are more than a knowledge-base, skill, or even a vocation, but intertwine around and through the sub-frame of the personality, neither totally fused nor easily separable.

In terms of my formation in psychotherapy, I have been something of a magpie and have held myself back from any commitment to a single approach. I use and mix terminology from different schools of thought and do so without shame because, at their specialised emergence, those same words were taken from discourses more or less prevalent at the time. If someone else's idea has worked its way into my brain in such a way that it seems to me to be either self-evident, or the product of my own reflection, then I hope that its progenitor might regard this as a compliment. And if I should stumble independently on an idea that someone has, unbeknownst to me, published elsewhere, then perhaps they can consider this, in the parlance of qualitative research, to be useful triangulation.

There is a chapter on the nature of evidence. It will explain why I waste as little time as possible on the game of "Simon Says". I try to minimise the use of references to justify what I am saying, but acknowledge direct quotes and inspirational sources, and convention dictates that I use a system of references to do so. There are some thinkers whose writing I understand so imperfectly that I cannot meaningfully either quote, or even acknowledge, them. Martin Heidegger would be a good example, whose name merely rang a bell for me until, in the late stages of preparing this book, I stumbled across *Being and Time* (Heidegger, 1927) in which he attempts to explain in a consistent form of words the phenomenon of *being* including *being with* another in this world.

Wilfred Bion would be another example. Psychiatric membership examinations included, in my time, multiple-choice questions that might mention Bion; the task being to pair his name with, say, "basic assumptions groups", rather than with "curative factors in groups", which should have been paired with Irvin Yalom. Later on this was fleshed out a little more, and we were encouraged to read about beta elements, alpha function, and suchlike. The overt consensus was that it was too difficult but the reality, in retrospect, was that we simply had too many other things to get on and do. The end result of this was a number of words floating in pairs without much in the way of context or meaning, so easily forgotten, and a degree of almost subliminally incorporated, genuinely valuable, under-appreciated ideas.

In this way I have been influenced by a very large number of people: Irvin Yalom, Carl Rogers, Fritz Perls, Eric Berne, Wilfred Bion, Sigmund Freud, Carl Gustav Jung, Melanie Klein, Michael Rutter … The list could go on and, rather like someone at a wedding who has made the mistake of naming the people I need to thank, I encounter a fearful certainty that I shall miss someone from the list and be disparaged for it. I could not hope to do justice to the task of clarifying the complex network of interacting influences that have contributed to my formation. I have decided not to pretend that I am more familiar or comfortable with these great thinkers than I am. Some of them I feel I know like old friends. Others seem more like eccentric and confusing acquaintances of my father (who was, as it happens, a Freudian analyst).

My understanding of the practice of psychotherapy started in medical school in a supervised peer group discussion of Anthony Storr's *The Art of Psychotherapy* (1979). The clinical giant that I find myself most frequently returning to is Donald Winnicott. He wrote in a language that I find does not leave me behind and is clearly about the world that I inhabit. Of Winnicott's writing, *Playing and Reality* (1971a) greets me with the greatest concentration of common ground. I realised, when reviewing the references for this book, that I had adopted a similar approach to summarising each chapter. I did this quite unwittingly, and this seems to me to be another instance of things that I believe myself to have observed or evolved turning up in his writing. It is rather like those early memories that, through frequent retelling, become more like something handed down than a genuine and personal memory.

I cannot say that I am tempted to explore these published and enduring thinkers with anything like academic rigour. If I were to prove capable of the task at all, it would take too long and would result in a different book altogether. My relative lack of time, or cognitive patience, is less of a hindrance in the clinical setting where, after all, one has to do something before the day is gone. I shall make a virtue of necessity and yield what I hope shall prove to be a reasonably considered product from a reflective clinician.

The convergence that I observe between the interests of philosophy, psychoanalysis, and the arts finally intersects with those of science, it seems to me, in clinical work. The strain of retaining the creativity in this tension will be evident in what follows. The fate of the protagonist in *Zen and the Art of Motorcycle Maintenance* (Pirsig, 1974) suggests that insanity can be the origin, or prove to be the result, of trying, Icarus-like, too hard in this endeavour. I trust that I can avoid this outcome by relaxing well before the creation of a perfect synthesis.

The references I provide, therefore, will have to double as a bibliography. They should give the reader both some inkling of which published material may have informed or inspired my thinking as well as some directions to explore if their imagination is captured—though like pebbles found on a beach, what one finds oneself is usually more convincing. I have left out all the textbooks and suchlike that went into my training and continuous professional development.

I am inclined to avoid attaching labels to myself and I am a poor adherent to any single cause. Even Quakerism, for me, is a lens rather than a club, though if you know or find out a little about Quakerism you will realise that much of my approach to *being with* could trace origins there. However, before you jump to any conclusion on my theism or lack of it, I shall venture right here and now a clearer definition than any I have attempted in the last twenty years. I shall describe myself as a moderately aggressive agnostic. You will find that this chimes solidly with the central idea of this book. I hope that this evasive allegiance and the fact that what I have to say is unlikely to be the product of my simply toeing any single party line may make it more, rather than less, convincing. It certainly makes it more adaptable; the origin being more the space that arises between me and my patient, than anything else.

Tom Burns in the introduction to *Our Necessary Shadow* (Burns, 2013, p. xiii) identifies change from one's norm as the hallmark of mental illness. This points to a crucial difference between child and adolescent psychiatry and its adult counterpart. Even if the adult can be considered to have a "norm" from which to differ, the child does not. Indeed, it may be the child's most important task, at a given moment in her development, to deviate emphatically from the norm that she has been living thus far. Another important difference is that the child brings into the consulting room his most important context, namely his parental system. The child and adolescent psychiatrist has to be fully aware that this may be simultaneously the child's chief support and the chief threat to his healthy development. Hence we must forge a treatment alliance with these guardians that is genuinely affiliative and at the same time cautious—even sceptical. Therapeutic intent, therefore, results in a necessary duplicity.

I have chosen "he" and "she" by a semi-random process. "He or she" is cumbersome and "they" is vague and intrusive. Wherever it was possible to use either gender I have tossed a coin to decide. I grew up through a period when the intellectual expression of feminism was in a particularly vociferous and unambiguous phase and I learned that the use of gendered pronouns both reveals and creates assumptions about role. I suggest that the reader who experiences confusion as a result of this do what they can to relax and enjoy it, emerging hopefully slightly less likely to expect a doctor/chief executive/naughty child to be male, an anxious patient/parent/nurse to be female, or the working or otherwise absent parent to be the father. It is important that we remain aware that we are likely to be using stereotypes in order to jump to conclusions, be ready for any corrective information, and move on.

Much of this book is about the therapeutic relationship. This need not necessarily be in the context of an agreed and established psychotherapy. I distinguish psychotherapy from therapeutic relationship, and distinguish each of those two from the generally supportive interpersonal relationship.

This introduction hopefully serves to usher us all from the waiting room of the book covers, up the stairs, and into my clinic room—a space in which to explore and elaborate upon what I am calling therapeutic attitude.

CHAPTER ONE

Being and being with

In the chapters that follow I shall describe what I believe the attitude of *being with* might look like throughout the patient's journey but, first, I must try to explain what I mean by *being with* someone.

When Szczeklik tells us that, "Being there is the doctor's ultimate duty," he is probably referring to the end stages of illness, but he is clear that the challenge to the doctor is most acute when there is no way to remove suffering (2005, p. 86). At these times, compassionate human presence is invaluable. Yet simply being there can be the biggest challenge of all. Not being able to help (much) is commoner than we would like to admit. We prefer to identify something in the patient's experience that we *can* change, than to admit that what she is suffering from is something that we cannot significantly alter.

I met many patients before I developed the ability to be myself in their presence, let alone the ability to be *with* them in the sense that I hope to explain. The latter, in particular, demanded of me the capacity to be more or less comfortable with my own feelings, thoughts, and reactions, and to manage them appropriately.

Meeting patients no doubt threw me off centre somewhat, but being pushed off centre is an important part of finding an equilibrium. My encounters with others have probably served rhythmically to draw my attention to the value of re-establishing my ability to *be*. In the last ten years or so I have found that patients and their families present less of a challenge in this regard, than do other elements of my work as a consultant psychiatrist, such as committee meetings, actuarial demands, service development, and suchlike. This is probably because I find the agenda relatively clear in the clinical encounter, with one party asking the other for help, and because the presence of the child is conducive to play.

There is no doubt that any confusion in the account that follows reflects a degree of confusion in my thinking. I excuse myself from hammering this out with ruthless precision and am inclined to the view that more would be lost than gained through elaborating in a technical or highfalutin way, or attempting to pin down the concepts to any greater degree. Words can be used to synchronise experience between people up to a point, but from that point on, further details result in the drawing of distinctions and the redevelopment of distance. Instead I shall consider this confusion to be an example of "potential space" and I shall value it as an opportunity to play (Winnicott, 1971a, pp. 126–129).

This potential space is uncertain, even in so far as it exists. It is there, yet is not there, or it might be. It is potential in this sense of potentially existing, as well as being a potent space, and one in which a person's potential begins to be realised. In this elusive space we play—and grow. If the potential space is too successfully defined, it ceases to be potential. In becoming actual it ceases to be.

So you are there, trying to understand. And here am I, trying to be understood. Between us something is developing. It has not yet taken shape and it does not yet bridge the gap between us. You may be already impatient or bored, but I am suggesting that we play in or with this space.

Perhaps it is the challenge of being with others that stimulates the development of our ability to be ourselves, and being *with* ourselves might be the training ground for both. Let us leave it there and move on. Hopefully the sections that follow will form stepping-stones in this primal confusion.

Having and doing

Erich Fromm made the argument for a less acquisitive approach to life: *being* in contrast to *having* (Fromm, 1976). This contrast and argument will seem familiar to most of us now though we have almost certainly become even more materially acquisitive than we were when he set the distinction out so eloquently. I shall take it for granted that you, the reader, agree that there are more important things to human existence than the acquisition of material wealth, though we should acknowledge that for many this may not be a self-evident truth.

There is not only having. We need to think about the distinction between having, doing, and being. In a sense, they are all ways of being. I shall also briefly explore being, being oneself, being with oneself, and being with another, in order to be able to continue, hopefully with the idea of *being with* in a clinical setting, which is the purpose of the exercise.

Making these distinctions is fraught with danger. I had a clear sense of what I meant by *being with* and did not think about it very much until I came to write this book. The problem is that, in putting it into the necessary words, it is easy to become distracted by the semantics and then get confused. I shall take these distinctions in turn and do what I can with them as briefly as possible.

Having and doing are of obvious importance when it comes to the ability to meet relatively basic needs. If one needs water one can walk to find it or one can pay someone to provide it. The same applies to shelter, warmth, and food. The ability for either wealth or activity to secure the meeting of needs of a less tangible nature is more tenuous and complex. We are familiar with the adage "money can't buy you love", and most of us are aware of the pitfall of slavishly performing to secure the admiration of another, though we often struggle to avoid it.

Having, once it exceeds the necessary modicum, may be rather like an addiction; acquisition satisfying a superficial need in the short term but leaving more profound and less understood needs unmet. Often it leaves us with an additional sense of having sullied ourselves in some way.

I suspect that, a little like a phobia of the dark that began through biological preparedness derived in a context where it was functional, a functional drive to obtain some degree of security in an insecure environment becomes exaggerated and compulsive. Excessive having and excessive doing are probably to do with some sort of insecurity.

Very often, in attempting to live a more virtuous and less acquisitive life, we launch ourselves into a life of doing, perhaps accumulating virtue or achievement credits instead of material wealth. Having and doing are not the same, but there are some parallels.

Being and doing

I am not convinced that there is a distinction between being and doing, the classification of *to be* as a verb suggesting that we cannot *be* without doing *something*, but I do think that it is useful to behave as though these two things are different, and in order to make sense of this book it will be essential to do so. I shall muddy the water first, and then let it settle.

When Winnicott said that the individual has "to reach *being* before *doing*" (1971a, p. 152), the emphasis might just as well have been on the word "individual". He went on to say that unless "I am" precedes "I do", the latter has no meaning. He acknowledges, though, the pre-separation, merged state of the baby-plus-mother or baby-plus-world and, in purely objective, mechanical terms we would probably all agree that the baby is *doing* things, such as crying, defecating, feeding, etc., before it has any sense of itself as a subject doing those things. I shall suggest that, for the objective baby to do anything, it has to *exist*. On the other hand, coming into existence could be regarded as the first thing that it *does*. Then, before it can be a subject in its own experience and action, it has to develop a sense of "I". It does this by an iterative process of being and doing, gradually accruing subjectivity along the way.

But in this book I am talking about clinicians who are hopefully at a much later stage of development. We have to assume a subjective state of "I"-ness, and in this world I find it useful to draw some sort of distinction between *being* and *doing*. An illustration may help to move us on.

My mother was not in the least materialistic, but she worked very hard as a single-handed rural general practitioner and then, after her retirement, worked very hard at a great number of other things. It seemed that it was only old age that gave her permission to simply *be* and, even then, she found it hard.

Anthony Storr wrote a short article in the *Oxford Medical School Gazette* in the 1980s entitled *Don't just do something, listen!* He made the point that it can often be very important, though difficult, to *not* do something, particularly when we are in the presence of hardship or worry and have cast ourselves in the role of helper. We do things to neutralise discomfort. If someone comes to us in discomfort a tension is created which it is our tendency to attempt to reduce.

Being, though, is not about not doing *anything*, which is probably impossible, but about being aware of what we are doing and then taking ownership, wherever possible and appropriate, of the choice to do or to not do. Our experience and action in the here and now become the focus of our open-minded and non-judgemental attention. Nor is it about abolishing automatic action, because there will be automatic actions that rightly remain so. Breathing would be one. It is sufficient that we become aware that some of the things we do are automatic and should probably remain so. Other activities, though, may have become automatic in a less helpful sense, and we should identify them as outcomes of choice and therefore amenable to choosing.

An ability to discern the shift from being to doing is a good way of protecting oneself from compulsive action.

Before leaving the doing mode of existence, there is the matter of how many things we try to do. I once attended a presentation by a practitioner of the Alexander technique. She spoke whilst juggling three ripe plums and told us that she was doing this partly so that we would remember her own talk over the others (I have remembered it, so far, for about thirty years), but also so that we would understand that it is easy to do two things at once, provided it is only two. If there is something that we really want or need to do, it is likely that we will do it better if we are not simultaneously and compulsively doing a large number of other things. Being able to reduce what we do in the moment is a way, not only of choosing what we do, but also of doing things properly.

Ways of being

Being is something I cannot help doing (*sic*). I believe I have a level of being that is the same as that of an animal, a stone, or the weather. Whether or not I *think*, I am. I can think as much as I like about my existence, but doing so does not make my existence any more real.

So much for *being*. I cannot avoid it, whatever I am doing, or whatever mode I am in. I shall return to *being* mode in a moment, but shall for the time being say that it is a state in which striving (after truth, action, attainment, etc.) is minimised. The Zen tradition has handed down the instruction "just sit". I suggest that the instruction for *being* mode is "just be". Because it doesn't come very naturally to us, it requires practice, and this contains a paradox that I shall come back to.

One can consider what it is to be oneself and to be with another. I shall slip past "being oneself" and suggest that there is some striving therein and that it is, therefore, not the same as "just being". If I can be anything other than myself (which the idea of being myself suggests) then the idea must involve things like sense of identity, image, expression, consistency, motivation, etc., and these are all judgements, actions, and concepts. In other words, they are about doing and thinking.

Incidentally, being a psychiatrist, like being anything else that contributes to our self-perception, quickly becomes more an example of clinging-on than of being. Being a specific thing is more like doing or having because it requires temporal stability.

We have left behind, then, both "being" and "being myself". Now for *being with*: I do not simply mean "existing in proximity to" because, like "being" this is of little interest to me in the current context. It is either inevitable, or its definition rests on physical measures of distance. Also I want to be able, if only briefly, to think about being with myself, and this would be meaningless unless it included more than simple physical proximity. When I talk about "being with" I am referring to being in *being* mode *in the company* of another. I shall return to this after a brief detour through two influential areas derived from Eastern spiritual philosophy and practice.

Mindfulness, the Tao, and a fresh breeze from the east

It is probably necessary for there to be a taboo on overt religion in a uniformly delivered health service, simply because of the power of words to divide people when adhered to with fervour. Alain de Botton has described rather elegantly how useful religious values could be if only the extrapolated fine print could be passed over or taken more lightly (de Botton, 2012). It is essential that the team pulls together for the sake of the patient population and if talking about a particular topic were to split or distract the team, then it would be better for it to be avoided. This is slightly ironic, as the religions, when they are not set against one another, share a number of values, perhaps most notably variations on a theme of altruism, which are particularly well suited to serving a culture of healthcare.

Mindfulness has made an interesting and welcome breakthrough, however. It can be described as the practice of a non-judgemental awareness of what you are doing from moment to moment, whether that be breathing, hearing, remembering, worrying, planning, etc. Despite its spiritual or religious connotations (it is broadly derived from Buddhist meditation), a predominantly scientific mental health community has adopted it, no doubt because it has been shown by methods that pass scientific muster to have outcomes of utilitarian value (Williams, Teasdale, Segal & Kabat-Zinn, 2007). The paradox is that the practice itself eschews the utilitarian motive. Mindfulness has been described as maintaining oneself in the *being* mode (Kabat-Zinn, 1991, p. 20). If one practices mindfulness in order to achieve some end, then one is thinking, trying, and future-oriented; one is neither non-judgemental, nor in the here-and-now. There are some things that you are more likely to have, the less effort you put into getting them.

The other "Eastern" influence that has impressed me and provided me with a tool is Taoism. Tao is "the way", not in the sense of a code of practice, but in the sense of inevitability, sometimes called the "watercourse way" (Watts, 1975). I am inclined to equate it with "god-or-nature" (Spinoza, 1994). The Taoist approach helps us in our attempts to understand something that seems essential and yet is elusive, and it does so by pointing out that efforts to capture the essence of running water in a bucket result in failure and disappointment. The opening words of the Tao Te Ching are usually translated along the lines of, "The Tao that is described is not the true (or eternal) Tao" (Mears, 1922, p. 22; Watts, 1975, p. 38–39). Time and again, I shall argue that our attempts to define, measure, and reproduce in specific terms what it is that we do have drawn us away from its most important and human aspect; in defining what we do we miss the point of what we do. Perhaps this is nothing more than a stating of the observer effect which applies from the cosmic to the human: if you observe or measure something, then you are likely to alter its nature.

Of these two ideas, both of which appeal to my thinking, it is mindfulness that I practice. I shall not attempt to teach it in this text, but can recommend it with few reservations. Its emphasis on the suspension of judgement has resonance elsewhere in mental health, for example, the curiosity and non-expert positions of systemic practice (Jones, 1993), and can, I think, usefully be expressed as "beginner's mind" (Suzuki, 1970).

Being with

I have described *being with* as being in the company of another. This other can be an idea as well as a person, and it can be helpful to think of that including oneself. One can meditate, or one can meditate *on* something. That something could be an idea or it could be a person. They may be in the room with me but, more importantly, they are within the realm of my mindful attention. I have them in mind.

The possibility of *being with* oneself is important in the therapeutic setting because we are all human, with failings that it would be hubristic to believe we could simply leave outside of the room. Being aware of one's self, with it's needs, fears, etc., is necessary, in my view, even if only to enable us to let those things be.

If one is to *be with* a number of things (including, for example, a patient) at the same time, it goes without saying that this will include conflicting viewpoints and interests. Valuing these without being judgemental—being able to hold them all in mind—is one of the reasons that a comfort with uncertainty and paradox is necessary. Mindfulness, because of its self-conscious unselfconsciousness, and its aim to be without aim, becomes, amongst other things, an exercise ground for the toleration of paradox. The clinician who practices mindfulness will be better able to maintain a therapeutic alliance with someone of strong and contrary views, and to engage with the living paradoxes that will be brought to them in their work. In turn they can enable the therapeutically necessary potential space.

I find mindfulness both a useful lubricant when things are stuck and an essential anchor when they move: anchor, lubricant, reminder, and training ground.

Abstinence

I have been talking about not doing. Not doing something when you are drawn towards doing it, rather like not having, amounts to abstinence. Abstinence is important in a therapeutic relationship because, although by no means all of the power lies with the therapist, it is the therapist's ethical and moral duty to exercise in the interests of the patient what power she does have. She must be able to be aware of and abstain from satisfying her own drives, or at least place them second. This is the case whenever power is exercised by one on behalf of another, but it is particularly so where the other is in a vulnerable state. My young patients are vulnerable from a multiplicity of angles. They may be in the habit of doing what they are told or they may be experimenting with what happens if they don't do what they are told. At the very least, powerful interests around them still believe that they should do what they are told. They may be in a developmentally immature state. By virtue of either acute or persistent trauma they may be even more psychologically and emotionally vulnerable than their peers. They are, in any case, relatively bereft of political, legal, and financial power.

The clinician treating a child must abstain not only from the obvious abuses of power that, as a public, we are periodically shocked to hear about, but also from the automatic and apparently virtuous use of power in a direction that is generally acknowledged to be helpful. It might be, for example, an important developmental task for the patient better to distinguish her own needs from the demands that others place upon her and take firmer possession of her actions towards getting those needs met. In that case it would be important for us to abstain from "helpful" action that took this responsibility and opportunity away from her. This is the sort of thing that can be difficult to explain to managers or commissioners of services, and to reflect in the design of patient-satisfaction questionnaires. It is sometimes more therapeutic to be unhelpful.

The ability to move freely but consciously and deliberately into and out of *doing* is essential to this kind of work.

Enlarging the sphere of mindful attention

Being with someone else is largely about including them in your sphere of attention in a non-judgemental and non-automatic way. Necessary prerequisites include the abilities to *be* and to *be with* yourself, each requiring you to abstain from self-gratification and automatism (the latter possibly including at times what your employer would call doing your job). It is important to be able to demonstrate to the person that you can continue to be with yourself whilst also being with him, and that you are capable of abstinence, in relation not only to your own selfish drives, but also in relation to various expectations placed on you by referrers, parents, employers, the public, and so on. Part and parcel of this is to abstain from making judgements about what the patient should or shouldn't do, feel or say. Later on I shall describe the importance at times of not diagnosing and not treating. When I do so, this is what lies behind it.

Mindful attention is a way of allowing something to exist without bringing it into existence by the act of looking for it. If I direct my attention to the ending, for example, or anything outside of what is happening now, I am *being* less, and thinking, judging, worrying, etc., more. I am less mindful. My actions and what I say are more likely to be driven by these external issues than by the process with my patient, and I am less able to be with them.

Having said this, it is important to acknowledge the necessity of enlarging the sphere of mindful attention even beyond *being with* the patient. I must be able to respond to urgent intrusions of outside life. In the next chapter, and in outright contradiction of my own article of faith that the subjective is as real as the objective, I have called these necessary intrusions "reality". I need to be capable of bringing into the room and into my attention, or sometimes my joint attention with the patient, matters such as information provided by others, the question of diagnosis, hypotheses about causation or remedy, or the future fact of ending and saying good bye.

Being silent

The importance of silence in *being with* becomes obvious when one considers its opposite. If neither of us were to stop talking we could hardly say that we had genuinely been in each other's company, let alone learned much about the other. Too much silence, though, can become a subtle form of bullying, particularly when one person is very used to it or is much the more powerful. I often explain to my patient the usefulness of some silence in allowing us to discover what matters. When I am silent with another I find I am more aware that there is a shared and an unshared component to our experience. When you are busy talking it is easy to believe in the illusion that you are carrying the other person's attention and experience with you. So the clinician needs to be comfortable with silence, not so as to persecute the patient with it but so that, if silence opens up, the clinician's mind is not immediately taken over by worries about what it means or what to do about it.

Being a psychiatrist

Radden and Sadler (2010) employ virtue ethics to remind us that characteristics are distinct from skills and may be more important. Virtue ethics alerts us to an important difference between *doing* psychiatry and *being* a psychiatrist. Doing psychiatry would involve asking the right questions, delivering good clinical advice, and even demonstrating the correct attitudes, where "right", "good", and "correct" are all up for debate, but are typically decided by a complex process of academic, professional, and popular dialogue. One of the correct attitudes is genuineness but, as Radden and Sadler argue, merely demonstrating the appearance of genuineness is not enough; it must be *genuine* genuineness. It needs to be more than an attitude, such as one might "strike". It has to be a quality. It is not sufficient to *do* psychiatry or therapy but it is important to *be* whatever it is to be a psychiatrist or a therapist. If I were looking for a psychiatrist for myself, I would not want one who is good at behaving *as though* she is interested in me. I would want her to be *actually* interested in me, even if only temporarily.

It hasn't escaped my own notice, and it may not have escaped yours, that I said that "striking an attitude" was not sufficient, having chosen for the title and theme of this book, *therapeutic attitude*. It is possible, however, to practice attitude and for it to become ingrained. One can become a therapist, nurse, doctor, psychologist, psychiatrist, etc. One of the values of the apprenticeship model of learning is that it encourages this process of getting the attitude under the skin. The point is that, by learning how to *do* the clinical work, in the presence of people who *are* practised clinicians, one *becomes* a clinician. Doing encourages being, and being enables one to do.

Children and adolescents are generally very adept at detecting what the fictional, but very real, Holden Caulfield (Salinger, 1951) would probably have called phony behaviour and, when they do so, it usually serves to put them off. Condescension is a particularly noxious manifestation of the phony because it denies so utterly the subjective agenda and drama (Miller, 1987) of being a child. The spirit of any young person who attends the clinic daring to hope that he might come through the encounter to a greater level of understanding of, and comfort with, himself, is likely to plunge in response to condescension. It is a shame when adults condescend to children in general walks of life, but it is particularly essential for the clinician to avoid any condescension towards their child patient.

Standing alongside

A good way to avoid condescension is to locate oneself metaphorically beside the child and on his level. This is helped if one can imagine the child's predicament (Taylor, 1985) in an externalised way (White & Epston, 1990). The clinician and the child can then position themselves beside one another in joined contemplation of the predicament. The young patient is confronted by a conundrum to which the solution is in no way obvious. The image of a Chinese puzzle comes to mind. The child senses that the puzzle is partly of his making and yet he has no recollection of his role in its construction. It is as though whilst in a fugue state or dream he, his family, school, and social circle constructed this elaborate and precarious structure that now blocks his path.

Imagine the young person's consternation were I to step in and start to push sticks of dynamite into the spaces, or haul energetically at one of the pieces. If he were to welcome this style of intervention, he would be wrong to do so. He should be pretty certain that I will not know straight away how to solve it, and he might have an instinctive sense that, for all its apparently alien nature and immovability, the structure could be vulnerable and that damage to it might entail damage to himself. Like a transitional object (Winnicott, 1971a, pp. 1–7) it was constructed or adapted by him. It has a place in the life of the child. In a sense it *is* the child (constructed by him, unknowing). It might recur. For all of these reasons it is better if the child is involved—and not just passively—in its deconstruction or its further and more functional adaptation.

So my position is alongside the child, looking at the conundrum, as though to say, "Is this what you would like us to think about?" As we begin to look at it together I might begin to spot aspects that he had not noticed. I might, on the other hand, get something wrong, or not know what to do. The child must know that I am fallible, but that I am comfortable with the idea of being fallible. In this way his own helplessness becomes less daunting. I need to be an expert in problems and their solutions, but not yet (and perhaps never) in *his* problem. I must also be an expert in not knowing and in waiting.

Compassion is an important feature of *being with*. This almost goes without saying when one considers the origins of the word compassion.

Of crucial importance in mindful meditation is the manner in which we return to the anchoring focus of our attention, be that the breath, or something else. This return must be in a spirit of graceful, welcoming companionship towards oneself. When I am working explicitly in a mindful way and I notice that my attention has wandered or is chasing thoughts, I use the image of putting my arm around my attention as I steer it back. In this way I am correcting, but kind to, myself.

In the same way that being alongside myself helps me to encourage my mindful *being* mode, so does being alongside the patient—*being with* them—help me to see things their way and offer a plausible and safe resource for them to use. My compassion towards myself and my errors or limitations gives them courage.

The compassionate challenge

A family has a culture, and so does a person. I don't just mean that a person belongs to a culture, but that they also have a culture personal to them. It is important not to do violence to this culture. When you travel to another country, provided you are not doing so in an insensitive and boorish way, you will learn how to enter a room. You do not know, at first, what the correct behaviour is, so you enter quietly and alert. You pay attention to what others are doing. You might watch for a moment before joining in. Some rudimentary but important social behaviours will occur to you, though you have never been told them. You will, for example, walk around the backs of chairs as much as you can to get to the empty chair, rather than cutting across the lines of sight and dialogue between others in the room. Meeting a family can be similar. In both situations a certain curiosity or naiveté (Dyche & Zayas, 1995) can be invaluable. This is the practice of cultural safety.

There is a Māori concept, *whakamā*, which refers to an emotional state something like shame. I was impressed to hear about it while working in New Zealand, which was where I was also introduced explicitly to the notion of cultural safety.

A white European doctor was working at a New Zealand hospice for the terminally ill when one of the Māori patients died. The doctor, along with the other Pākehā staff, was invited to the *tangi* where, as is the custom, the welcoming family and the visitors each elected one of their number to make a short speech, in each case followed by a song. Singing, typically in rousing harmony, is an integral part of Māori community life. When it came to the visiting professionals, there was no confident singer in their midst and they timorously started a hymn remembered, at least in part, from their school days. They stood, gathered, but feeling almost naked in their shame, as they offered their quavering voices. Within a few bars and almost as though from a single thought the relatives of their patient joined in and the nurses and doctors felt themselves lifted and held by the mourners.

In the act of helping someone it is important not to undermine or diminish them. In her book about *whakamā*, Joan Metge (1986) quotes the description of a person helped in their *whakamā* by the act of someone putting an arm around or standing alongside them. Her book is a study of cultural sensitivity, sensitivity which, incidentally, might well include not being too soft but rather showing some confidence in the robustness of the other. The challenge of the Māori greeting is partly a vote of confidence in the other. "We know you have metal. Show it to us!" Charity can undermine.

So being with someone does not necessarily mean being nice to them, agreeing, or nodding sagely. (One parent took up the suggestion of getting some therapy for himself and came back describing his therapist as "the nodding dog".) Being with someone may require some combat and robustness or, as Karin Grossman and others put it in the context of paternal sensitivity towards toddlers, "sensitive challenging" (Grossmann et al., 2002).

Travelling alongside

It probably goes without saying that *being with* someone who is on a journey involves travelling with them. Various metaphors come to mind but I have to acknowledge that, for all my compassion and empathy, the dangers I face as I journey with my patient, whilst real enough, are entirely different from their own. Whether they are greater or less is debateable, but they are not the dangers under consideration. For this reason the metaphor of the mountain guide or the marine pilot are not so appropriate.

When I contemplate my medical role I often return to the idea of the boatman on the River Styx. This seasoned traveller and guide has a specialist role when people need to visit Hades for any reason. These people may pour their troubles out to the boatman as he ferries them across, or they may sit in silence, but they will be grateful that he has been there before, and will be anxious to know that he will wait to ferry them back when their task is done. This analogy works quite well. We don't know how the boatman behaves. He may be chatty or taciturn and the crossing may be long or short. He may or may not advise people in their tasks on the other side and we are not confident that he accompanies any of the overland journey—quite possibly not.

I do not use my anatomy training, and I have long since left what experience I had of internal examination behind me, but the fact that I have crossed these taboo thresholds, held back the emerging baby's head, certified the dead, summoned and consoled the relatives, seen someone's insides and then looked them in the eye, equips me for pretty well any task to do with the human condition. I believe that my patients sense this. Perhaps accompanying my cheerful greeting is enough of the weary traveller, the wounded healer, or the eyes that have seen the beginning and end of life. Or perhaps these qualities were something that my patients need to project onto someone and the letters after my name make me a likely candidate. Either way, it enables me to be with them in particularly daunting situations. When the monsters rise from the deep I may be less likely than some to retreat into action. This may be fantasy, or magical thinking, but what else would parents mean when they say that someone looks "too young to be a doctor"? In both childhood and mental health work one travels between reality and phantasy. In a land of make-believe, something like a magician comes in handy. "Yes", I might say, "I can do all those things, but they are not required just yet."

Time

Everything we do is an opportunity to demonstrate our position alongside our patient as a skilled and experienced—but most importantly human—companion, unafraid of being with ourselves and unafraid of being with the patient and his predicament, even if this at times means admitting that we do not have a solution to it, or even fully understand it. In order to foster this confidence in me, the process, and ultimately the patient, I must be able to temporise.

If we don't know what to do right now, and provided it is safe to do so, it would be worth letting a little more time go by. We can then regroup and the way forward may be clearer. It is nearly always safe to wait a little. Sometimes it is necessary to wait indefinitely.

The adults in the child's system are quite likely to be expressing a degree of impatience. In the project of becoming oneself there is no meaningful time limit. Does a child need to become herself fully before her year-eleven exams? No. In fact failing one's exams, or letting them slip by this year may be a very important step towards becoming one's self. It may be important to find some internal motivation for passing exams before taking them. Not infrequently someone comes to me with chronic fatigue, unable to maintain a full day at school. Any attempt to do so is followed by an exhaustion that sets her further behind in her efforts. It is obvious that nothing short of a miracle (we call them miracles because they offer something better than we expected from chance and we don't know how they happen) will enable this young person to be firing on all cylinders in time for her exams later in the year. These young people are typically intelligent, as are their parents, and yet not one of them seems to be able to entertain in mind or discourse an outcome that is practically inevitable. Efforts to avoid acknowledging this unacceptable likelihood bring it even closer. It is like an addiction. Milan Kundera called it vertigo (1984, p. 60). I have noticed it when cycling—the eye catches something on the ground and our desire to evade seems to impel us towards it.

As soon as failure (against prior expectations) is acknowledged as a possibility—not a hypothetical possibility that must be avoided at all costs, but a real possibility—one of a number of possible outcomes, each of which leads on to some sort of future, the year after and the year after that—the task and timetable suddenly become more flexible and attainable, as though a world of possibilities had opened up. Some things become more possible when you stop trying to guarantee them.

A girl of fifteen presented with chronic fatigue. Partway through this process of adjusting expectations, her parents discovered a privately provided miracle cure that removed her symptoms. She and her parents were delighted. Several months later she returned with depressed mood and ideas of self-suffocation. I was able to discharge her after a further half a dozen monthly appointments, minus her depression and suicidal ideas, but still with some frustrations around family relations and self-image. I don't now if the two things—the fatigue and the work she had to do in understanding and transforming her depression—were linked, but I think that they probably were.

Being with several

As I said in the introduction, "it may be the child's most important task, at a given moment in her development, to deviate emphatically from the norm that she has been living thus far". There has to be, in my view, a spirit of rebellion in the child and adolescent mental health professional. I am all for happy families, but not families with an appearance of being happy, the maintenance of which is at the expense of the healthy development of a child. I shall not foment rebellion for the sake of it, but I shall question assumptions. I think I have found the safest way to do this is to be open to any possibility. There is a relationship between this and both the paradox of strategic family therapy and motivational interviewing as used, for example, in the approach to addiction. If a child wants to leave the parental home and live elsewhere at the age of fourteen, the best way to encourage her determination might be to oppose it. I will assume, therefore, that it could be the most sensible and safe thing to do. This might be taken by the parents as a suggestion that they are abusing their daughter. This is not what I mean, and I need to make that clear to them. What I mean is that the child has made a suggestion that should be taken seriously and judged on its merits. What are the possibilities and what are their pros and cons? What might be necessary?

The child's voice, and even more so at times, the adolescent's, is frequently either unheard or is heard and discounted. I shall be with him in discovering what he has said or wanted to say and encouraging its exploration. I hope I can also pick up the plaintive cries of the more passive parent, or the forgotten sibling, but my patient is the child. Having stated this fierce loyalty I shall immediately confuse it. Winnicott quotes himself as having said that "there is no such thing as a baby" (1957, p. 137). He was referring to the relational dyad of mother-and-baby. The same sort of thing is true in a clinical or developmental context later on. There is no such thing as a child-patient, or at least it is not helpful to *be with* the child without also being with his caregiving context. This would most typically be his parents, but should extend to embrace other aspects of his context. In the context of paediatric-liaison psychiatry, for example, there would be no such thing as a child but, rather, a child-and-treating-medical-team. Holding this context in mind, as well as the child, and knowing that one is, to some extent, treating both or all, can mean at times supporting rebellion in one part whilst embracing the whole. Indeed, supporting the idea of rebellion can be a powerful way of supporting actual cohesion.

There is another aspect to my being with the child or adolescent. It is assisted by the power that comes with being a doctor and a senior member of the team. Later I shall describe the importance of withholding both diagnosis and treatment. There is an element of childhood play or adolescent non-compliance to this and I think that what may be happening, apart from providing the young person with some time and space in which to explore meanings free from the pressure of the adult world, is some modelling of play or rebellion on my part. I need to do this whist simultaneously being the adult, or the society, that wants certain things of this child. It is as though I am saying that the adults, including the adult in me, want to carry out this investigation, or embark on this treatment, but that the child or adolescent in me is resisting. I can allow this to play out between the adult and the child *in me*, with my patient incorporating *her* own meanings and wishes as they emerge. There is a motivational interviewing aspect to this also, in that I am taking both sides of the argument—for and against a certain course of action—and in this neutral position I can facilitate the young person finding an expression of her own wishes. I can demonstrate a sort of accelerated maturation to them, in which my internal rebellious child, having gained expression and been taken seriously, can relinquish its reactive position and contemplate the demands of the adult world with greater equanimity and openness, possibly then to accept some of the demands being made.

Sometimes, of course, some value or expectation of the outside world simply needs to be brought to bear. This is likely to be more acceptable to the young patient if he can see that I have been open to alternatives. It is the capacity to be with the patient at the same time as the values and expectations of the adult world that is needed.

One further analogy may help here. How many of us have been in the situation of holding a conversation with an adult while a young child clamoured for our attention? Generally it is best not to ignore the child for long, but nor is it helpful or polite to immediately turn one's full attention to the child. Typically we will instinctively do something that indicates to her that she is in the room too; she has been noticed and will be attended to. Either an unfocused but welcoming glance that acknowledges her without immediately inviting, or a hand on the shoulder as we continue to talk—or a brief and very clear word explaining that we will want to know what she is saying in a minute when we have finished what we are doing (usually it cannot be much more than a minute).

Now imagine that, instead of the clamouring child, it is the values and expectations of the outside world that are clamouring. I must not ignore them, but nor must I be too distracted. I can be with the adult and with the child. I can be with the subjective or the rebellious *and* with the hard facts and legal requirements.

Summary
• The ability to be of use to a young person with mental health problems requires, as well as good professional training and support, the ability in the practitioner to prioritise *being* over *doing*. • It is probably not helpful to become too exercised with the distinction between these, but behaving as though the distinction exists enables the avoidance of premature action and judgement, and allows a therapeutic space to open up with the patient. • Mindfulness can provide a useful approach to establishing this ability. • The metaphors of the experienced guide standing and walking alongside can be helpful in conceptualising the attitude. • The capacity to abstain, contain, temporise, and equivocate are as important as the ability to discriminate and act, but are generally neither understood by commissioners nor taught during professional training, though they seem to be intuitively grasped and appreciated by the child. • There is "no such thing" as a child divorced from their caregiving, developmental context. • Paradox abounds, and the ability to live with and even encourage paradox is a therapeutic necessity. • Do not panic.

CHAPTER TWO

The intrusion of reality

A trainee psychiatrist was aware that a total solar eclipse was to occur during a therapy session with an adult patient. The sessions started according to method and proceeded along prescribed lines until a change in the ambient light drew their attention to the outside world. After the briefest of discussions the pair went out to join a gathering of people around the hospital entrance. The light was unforgettable—eerie and metallic—and an uncertain number of minutes elapsed before, through some process of consensus, they returned to the clinic and concluded their session.

A great number of assertions could be made about reality, and most of them would be to some extent values-based. I could assert, for example, that subjective reality is as real as objective, and that your reality and mine are equally valid perspectives. In some areas of clinical practice it is undoubtedly crucial to accept the reality of subjective experience. There is no forward mileage to be gained from denying the reality of pain, for example. However, some realities have a way of exerting an unquestionably concrete influence. We cannot survive for long on subjective realities alone.

Hierarchy and reality

Take the fire alarm. The importance of responding is less obvious when the fire drill is practised so frequently that it has become an exercise in herding, and a systematic unlearning from experience (or the story of the boy who cried "wolf"). Nevertheless, it would be appropriate to give the need for a swift response to the fire alarm some sort of hierarchical ascendancy. Typically people seem to pause for a moment before responding, suggesting that the response is not an automatic one, but willed. These people have not entirely forgotten the wolf story. The possibility of competing dangers are still being weighed up, perhaps, but my suggestion is that the need to confirm the agency of one's being takes hierarchical precedence over the simple perpetuation of physical existence.

Being with the patient and maintaining a certain detachment from the outside world must not prevent an ability to respond appropriately to these kinds of realities. It is a little like the phenomenon of driving without conscious awareness of what one is doing, yet applying the brakes with alacrity and skill when someone enters the road unexpectedly from the side. There must be some degree of attunement, in the here-and-now, to the practical realities of the outside world. This is necessary, but it should not allow us to demote the subjective process. When I am driving I may be doing so on autopilot. More consciously I may be talking to a friend, listening to the radio, or thinking about something. Less consciously I am monitoring the road ahead and around me for surprises. Each of these levels is important and there may be no straightforward hierarchy between them, though I would suggest that the driving skills, automatic and subliminal though they may be, take the ascendancy. It is quite a miraculous skill, when you think about it. High-level firearms training may involve being alert to a figure suddenly appearing in a doorway, interposing between detection and response the assessment required to distinguish a mother carrying a baby from a combatant carrying a weapon. In just the same way I should swerve for a human on a dual carriageway, but probably not for a dog. On a Monday morning I smile and continue talking when the fire alarm goes off, but not on a Thursday.

In the same way, in a clinical session, there should be several levels of alertness running simultaneously and directed towards:

1. the here-and-now of the patient (*being with*);
2. all the relevant clinical issues (questions of diagnoses and mental state, treatment options, and clinical dangers such as suicidality, uncontained regression, side effects of medication);
3. the time constraints of the session;
4. the possibility of the fire alarm or another acute and pressing matter of safety.

A clinical example of the firearms training analogy could be the necessity of listening with genuine interest and compassion as a mother describes the problems of her child whilst at the same time remembering that there have been concerns about exaggerated and inappropriate illness behaviour on her part. Keeping this history in peripheral vision, alert to it but not responding, is a clinical skill. To butt in and challenge her perspective in too trigger-happy a way would be inappropriate. Incidentally, the mother's own behaviour in relation to her child's health reflects, in turn, a tendency towards shooting at anything that moves.

For my patient, discerning the realities that can and cannot be escaped, and responding to them accordingly, may be the central task. Despite the value that I personally place on nurturing a sense of self, autonomy, and authenticity in the developing individual, I know that that person needs to live in what, for want of a better description, we call the "real world". This may be a universally acknowledged reality or she may need to live in and adapt to a world, the reality of which is largely constructed by her parents. On one hand I want her to pay attention to her own wants and instincts; on the other, I want her to adapt to certain albeit unwanted pressures from the environment. As is so often the case, I am walking a line: I cannot in good conscience encourage her to ignore the material pressures of the world, yet were I to say to her anything along the lines of "get real!" I would risk rupture of the therapeutic alliance.

The assumption that "concrete" reality should always take precedence over subjective reality when it comes to choosing what to do would be a false one. People have died for their beliefs. Probabilities can come into play: the low probability of a concrete loss might be outweighed by the high probability of a subjective benefit. Describing these different realities as being arranged in a hierarchy, though, invites comparison with the imposition of one individual's reality over another's.

It might be that the imposer believes that they have material or moral right on their side, or they may simply be bullying. We could almost feel as though we were being bullied by the fire alarm or, even, the fire. This may be why I wait for just a short while before responding to the fire alarm—to make sure that I am not simply being bullied into action.

Inescapable and ungraspable realities

Clearly, then, there are different realities, arranged hierarchically, in terms of our adaptive need to respond to them. The hierarchy can change in different settings and timescales, and it is not necessarily mirrored by any simple hierarchy in the level of our consciousness of those realities, or their tangibility.

There are realities that one "cannot escape" and realities that one "cannot grasp". Each can intrude in a different way. Keeping them "in mind" (for want of a better phrase) and responding proportionately and therapeutically is no mean feat.

The therapeutic importance of subjective truth

In my more depressed moments I wonder if this book, and indeed much of my professional career, amounts to a sort of fiction. It may be that I am deluded or misguided in believing that I have been of any use to my patients over all of these years. That many of them have said "thank you" can give little in the way of lasting comfort at these times. Perhaps those patients were just being polite, or they might have been as deluded as I was, surfing on the cresting rollers of my grandiosity. But this would be depressive thinking on my part, particularly if I generalised it to *all* of the work I had done. I can repair my mood and thinking and console myself with the likelihood that someone was helped, and that my instincts are unlikely all to be deluded. Even so, when I have done this I remain vulnerable to the accusation of an inability to prove that what I have done was genuinely useful. The fact that there are truths that are apparently "graspable" can undermine the validity of those that are not.

At these times all I can do is to fall back, on the one hand, on my belief and, on the other, a certain rational argument. The former is presumably made possible by an accident of my nature and upbringing. I have a sense that some things are true or valid, because they appear to me to be self-evident. Why would they appear self-evident? Perhaps because I have seen a multitude of subliminal hints or pointers that suggest their validity to me. I was delivered into the world and brought up in such a way that I am able to continue to believe in the validity of my experience. I am not saying that I don't change my mind or that I cannot be persuaded. What I think I am saying is that I am built in such a way that I give credence to things that come from within myself, as well as things that come from without. This might be a form of grandiosity but most of the time I consider this to be a healthy source of resilience.

The rational argument goes something like this: to be a curative or therapeutic agent it is essential for me to believe that "the way things are" is not an inevitable given. I simply have to believe that, however bleak the situation or experience of my patient, things can become better than they are. If his situation seems objectively bleak, then I cannot cynically weave a web of conviction around him alone. It has to work for us both. In the therapeutic world there is a moral imperative for the "way things are" to be held at bay while the "way things could be" is given a leg-up. In other words, my work only makes sense if I can allow the hypothetical some degree of ascendancy over the actual.

In another chapter I look at this from a slightly different angle. The "importance of uncertainty" will be another way of looking at the "intrusion of reality".

I have undermined my own argument by using the word reality to denote objective reality, as opposed to subjective reality, implying that the first has some sort of ascendancy. Frankly, I think my doing so reflects the fact that, whist I am capable of believing and arguing that subjective reality is of equal importance—or that ultimate non-attachment, in the Buddhist sense, is a viable and even theoretically preferable approach to life—I live my own life as though this were not the case, and actions speak louder than words. I have held on to a job that at times causes me despair because of the financial security that it provides for my family and me. I pay my income tax, even though a proportion of it is spent on things of which I do not approve, and so on.

Similarly, in the clinical world I diagnose attention deficit hyperactivity disorder if the currently prevalent diagnostic criteria are met, even though I regard it as part social construct, part spectrum of physiological hardwiring, part behavioural learning, and all with no demonstrably objective cut-off. I do so because refusal would be to, a) deny a certain culture or consensus, b) expose me to palpable dangers, however philosophically unsound their underpinning, and c) consign a child to an ongoing misery of academic and social failure and the risk of exclusion, substance misuse, and other downstream difficulties, when I might hold the key to a relatively risk-free way to improve this child's situation and outlook.

Values-based practice

It must be acknowledged that some objective realities have to hold greater sway than others. It would be ridiculous to attempt to live life as though gravity did not exist. It would be unwise to live as though theft were not a punishable offence. But when it comes down to realities that base their validity on ninety-five per cent confidence intervals in meta-analyses of disparate trials carried out on disparate individuals, it becomes clear that some subjective realities, beliefs, or values might correctly have the ascendancy. I shall come back to the cultural hegemony of statistics in another chapter. Suffice to say here that it represents one way of looking at things. Social, family, and individual values are another.

Each can see the other as an intruding reality. Family values might prevent the use of an evidence-based treatment. On the other hand, much as one might like to hold to the idea that one should avoid the use of medication, it might be hard to ignore convincing data pointing to its use after prolonged and fruitless efforts with a psychological approach.

Bill Fulford and others have explored and set out the idea of values-based clinical practice (Fulford, Peile & Carroll, 2012). They observe that values abound and that they are typically not explicit. Often we act forcefully in a certain direction without being conscious of the values that underpin our practice.

Just because the scientific community would translate a collection of experiences and phenomena into a diagnosis on the basis of diagnostic criteria, and then extrapolate this to a treatment plan, the clinician and the patient should not be mandated to do so. The importance of a widely accepted values-based approach is illustrated by the likely scenario without it, in which legal, professional, and public bodies would be inclined to think that failure (*sic*) to establish and act on such a plan amounted to negligence on the part of the clinician or neglect on the part of parents. Without a values-based ethos, the values—tacit or explicit—of a specific community or mindset hold too much sway.

A clinical team, meeting weekly to sift through referrals, was responding to the urgency of each case, placing the less urgent on a waiting list to enable more urgent cases to be seen within a fortnight. A member of the team would telephone the referrer or the family to clarify the situation if it were unclear, and patients put "on hold" were instructed to contact the team if the situation were to deteriorate. The consultant on the team was approached by trust management with a request to see a given patient because they were approaching the thirteen-week waiting limit. The consultant's reply was that referred patients would continue to be seen according to clinical urgency.

"Our services should be delivered in a timely fashion." I have heard this many times at strategy meetings and the like and sometimes I have questioned it. It is little more than a sound bite. Leaving aside the ambiguity of the word *timely*, one should at least make an effort to consider the values that come lower or higher in our hierarchy. Which values are being shouldered away by haste? Is *timely* more important than *effective*, for example, or *acceptable* to the patient? The speaker would then admit that she was talking about *effective* and *acceptable* treatments being given in a timely way. Then there is *affordable*. How much are we, as a nation, prepared to pay for the timely delivery of these treatments? It goes on. More honestly we should be saying, "I shall see patient x as soon as possible, bearing in mind her own priorities, the practical and financial circumstances, the likely improvement to be achieved by my seeing her, and any patients who need to be seen more urgently." The point I am making is that, because assumed values so easily become invisible to us, we can be aware only of the values currently either trending or controversial. Ten years ago I hardly ever heard the word "timely". It emerged along with a number of other words like "responsive" and phrases such as "joined up". Pushed to the front, they "glisten", and hard-pressed services join a gold-rush to lay claim to them. As we clamour to agree or argue over whether a service is provided in a sufficiently timely way, we lose sight of the hierarchy of values that inform, or used to inform and arguably should inform, what we do. We lose sight of them and, neglected, they slide down the hierarchy. It is a case of the tail wagging the dog—our unthinking practice defines our values, rather than the other way round.

Sadly, even "values-based" can become a trending value. This would be excellent news, provided it were genuine values-based practice that trended, rather than merely the term. What makes a service values-based is not the fact that choices are informed by values—that is always the case—it is the fact of the values and their influence on choice being made explicit. Nor is it sufficient to set out a list of popular buzz values, claim them to be one's own, and then state that one is practising values-based medicine. It may well be that our services should be "timely" and "evidence-based" but this would not make them any more or less values-based. One has to be alert, in the here-and-now clinical encounter as well as in the boardroom, to the values of the individual patient, as well as those of one's self, colleagues, employers, society, etc.

Values-based practice should be seen as an equal partner—at least—to evidence-based practice. The "at least" is important. It is only in deference to the current cultural *value* placed on empirical evidence and measurable gain that I hold back from putting the case more strongly. Ironically, it is because of the immense *value* that we place on the empirical (rather than, say, the spiritual or aesthetic) that we have it on a pedestal, and we have forgotten that it was value that put it there. In a tail-wagging way it has acquired the appearance of a dominant partner. If we are to practise healthcare responsibly we need to develop the awareness and skills required to elicit and work with values. If we do not pay attention to values, they play a stealth game.

Reconciling opposites

When we consider the empirical/objective and the values-based/subjective, we can see that each is a reality that can intrude on the other. How do we reconcile these pairs? Some may squirm or baulk at reference to the concept of Yin and Yang because of the exposure they endured in the sixties and seventies and the embarrassment with which we seem to have turned aside from the optimism of that era. But Yin and Yang are unavoidable, whether or not we choose to label them in that way: up and down, light and dark, soft and hard. Our lives are strung between opposites: birth and death, labour and relaxation, misery and exultation.

All creation begins with a splitting; the light from the dark, matter from not-matter, mitosis or meiosis. This separation can be seen also in the rising of the smith's hammer, the drawing of the bowstring, the intake of breath. What each of these analogies illustrates is the essentially cyclical nature of progress, or passage through time. It does not finish when the separation is "reconciled" because the separation is immediately reinstated, ready for the next reconciliation.

I have never been satisfied with the idea that the Kleinian "depressive position", itself described in ambivalent terms, is to be overcome. The depressive position is an achievement, a realisation, if not an acceptance, that the splitting of things into good and bad cannot be a lasting solution. It is the hammer and the anvil when the hammer has fallen. But it seems clear to me, and I think can be implied from Melanie Klein's writing (Mitchell, 1986), that there is a sort of meta-depressive position, which is less depression and more like compassion, with sadness and hope mingled, reflecting the fact that even the reconciliation is undone and redone, undone again and redone again.

When I speak, then, of the union or reconciliation of opposites, I am not talking about an end state, but an ongoing and cyclical process, itself in partnership with its opposite. Nevertheless, it is important to address ways in which this reconciliation takes place.

Because we reproduce sexually we are (and not only metaphorically) sandwiched between male and female. We are what holds them together and we do so within and threaded through our selves and our existence. Each of us is the embodiment of the holding-together of two. We may call them opposites if that makes them easier to conceptualise, but they are *the* two.

We cannot escape the fact that we are the product of our mother and our father. Often one—let us say our mother, but it is not always this way round—is the more tangible and present of the two; the father either a more shadowy or a more intermittently tangible figure, sometimes absent altogether and only guessed at, sometimes harder to grasp because of some repellent qualities he has, sometimes simply busy, nearly always yearned for, though often in a complex and shunning way. I say all this, not to reinforce a stereotype, but to strengthen the analogy that I am about to make.

When reconciling dyadic partners, like subjective and objective reality, we could think of them as mother and father (possibly respectively). They may be mortal enemies or they may be irrepressible lovers. Lyra's parents, Lord Asriel and Mrs Coulter, in the first book of Pullman's *His Dark Materials* trilogy, *Northern Lights* (1995), were both. We shall die before we achieve it, but our task, as children, however impossible, repellent or addictive, is to *embody* and *express* the union or reconciliation of these two. Sometimes it will make sense to us but often not. We continue anyway. We need them both and even when one of them is not "in the picture" we know they are somewhere and relevant.

When parents are at odds with one another, what I would hope, for the sake of the children, is for them to respect one another's contributions, take each other seriously, communicate, and pay attention to the individual needs of the child. Each parent demonstrates an ability to cope with the intrusion of reality represented by the existence of the other parent.

What I have said above may be summarised as follows: objective and subjective realities can be regarded as two parents: even if we are living with one of them, the other is important.

The intrusion of politics

I will not be alone in considering it important to abstain from exercising any kind of political values in the therapeutic encounter. Unfortunately even this can amount to a political position. Valuing individualism is not the same as valuing all individuals equally, and valuing all individuals equally appears to run the risk of eradicating individuality. The paradoxical—and impossible—position for me as a clinician is that I want the world for my individual patient and yet, as potentially the whole world could be my patient, none of them can have it. It is very like the paradox of parenthood in which the parent wants to give each of her children her full attention.

The solution, for the clinician, is to be found in the boundaries around appointments. If you start and finish on time and don't cancel appointments then, during the time allocated to your patient, she can be your topmost priority. Even then there will be pressures lobbying for your favour: family factions, individual happiness, education, and suchlike.

Placing the patient's developmental agenda above any other is, itself, a political position. What is more, it has its opponents, though they might be reluctant or unwitting in their opposition.

At this point I put aside my penchant for equivocating and propose the following manifesto: I approve of that which helps the developing child in his achievement of individuation, agency, and authenticity, and I consider anything that comes in the way of those to be a hostile incursion (albeit frequently well meant), including the expectation that my patient be helped towards fitting into society. I would like them to fit into themselves first and foremost.

I used to assume that fostering individuation and authenticity was my job and was what I was being paid for, but I have recently come to realise the extent to which this may not be the case. In the last few years a ghastly realisation has dawned on me: the question, *"Is it my purpose to support the individual in finding an authentic expression of themselves, or is it to turn them into a conforming and productive unit of society?"* has failed to elicit the clear and unambiguous answer that I had hoped for. It remains my steadfast view that I am here for the former purpose, but the question was begged the moment one person paid for the treatment of another and it becomes more pressing in a shrinking economy. Increasingly the machinery of state of which, as a publicly funded clinician, I am a cog, behaves as though the purpose is to get children back to school, back to sleep, back on the pavement, etc. It may be that the patronage of subversion was a luxurious bubble that has burst.

When I started studying clinical medicine I realised that, for me, there was little point in prolonging life if its quality was poor. To my mind the quality of life can only be meaningfully assessed subjectively, and has always required some element of self-actualisation or authenticity. The false selves that Winnicott described, emerging out of a premature requirement for compliance or imitation, might be ways of *being*, but they would not be very good ways of being *oneself*. I shall remain of the view that being a clinician is to nurture true selves, and that when clinicians serve the state they become dangerous. The state must continue to take the risk of fostering its professional children, knowing that all children turn against their parents at some time but bearing in mind that things generally work out in the end. If the state fails to maintain this degree of maturity then I foresee genuine therapy becoming a covert activity, like non-conformist churches following the English Reformation, practised in caves and on hillsides.

The intrusion of fantasy

In discussing the intrusion of reality we stumbled upon the concept of risk. Risk is no fantasy. Risk is real. It is the absence of risk that is the fantasy and we need to bear this in mind when we weigh practical realities against values, aspirations, and other intangibles. By noticing risk we are ourselves at risk of becoming phobic, as I shall outline in Chapter Three. We become addicted to the notion of a life devoid of risk. We devote our time and resources to the eradication of the negative instead of cherishing the positive. A clinician whose task it might have been to alleviate the worst of suffering and then turn the patient's attention towards a more hopeful horizon, is forced to knuckle down to the task of cleansing the Augean stables.

This fantasy of freedom from risk appeals to the public. We are familiar with the restriction of freedoms in order to reduce risk in the interests of national security. What may be less obvious is the restriction of clinical freedom in the pursuit of risk elimination, and the knock-on restriction of individuation and healthy development.

The existence of risk is a reality that appears to be such an unwelcome intrusion into our lives that we are inclined to respond with a concerted attempt to eradicate it altogether. We must be alert to this sort of fallacious thinking: the fact that something exists and is undesirable does not mean that its eradication should become the focus of our efforts. The fantasy of a life without risk is a siren call that could lead us onto the rocks of more covert and greater risk.

Paying the piper

The therapeutic venture becomes instantly more tenuous and complex when one person pays for the treatment of another. The economic powerlessness of children is an intrusive reality and renders this necessary. I am not sure which results in the more treacherous terrain: funding by parents or funding by the state. In the latter case the government or the taxpaying public pay and healthcare commissioners are the trustees of that process. Parents who bring their child, whether or not they miss work in order to do so, almost invariably invest significantly in the process also. There are thus several relatively powerful interests, some of them immensely powerful, paying for the treatment of the child. Each could be expected to seek some level of satisfaction in the outcome.

The French child psychoanalyst Françoise Dolto encouraged, from certain of her young patients, a symbolic payment, perhaps a stone or an old bus ticket (Dolto, 1987). The wisdom of this approach lies in its endorsement of the child as patient whose acceptance or refusal of the session requires expression and acknowledgement independently from their attendance which is, after all, in the hands of their parent. It might also, in a symbolic way, invest the child with greater power vis-à-vis the aims of the treatment. I doubt if many clinicians explicitly follow

Dolto's example. It is my belief, though, that the child does bring a gift. Anything laboured over and brought forth needs to be treated to some extent as a gift. To my mind, the genuine and sincere involvement of the child patient is sufficient to demand my own genuine and sincere involvement in exchange. If they bring themselves, then so should I, and they should be the protagonist in their own process.

Which tune to play

In a material and economically shrinking world these powerful investors in the child's treatment become more insistent. There was a time when doctoring was generally considered by definition to be a useful enterprise and the doctor was trusted to exercise her skill and expertise diligently, adroitly, sympathetically, and efficiently. It was sufficient for the state to employ the right numbers of a certain kind of clinician and then let them get on with it. The clinician in that position could interpose herself between the child and these powerful interests. It was possible, if necessary, to subvert these state and parental interests in the individual interest of the child. Sometimes, of course, both sets of interests were satisfied—the child who realised that he did not need to go to school found it easier to do so than he had imagined.

It seems only reasonable, now that there are fewer tax-payers' pounds available for the purchase of mental health care, to make sure that each pound is spent well. There is a difficulty here, though. The piper has to play a tune that the paymaster approves of and can hear. This is the other side of evidence-based medicine. I must provide evidence that I am doing something worthwhile. Problems abound. Do they measure the time I spend at work, the hours I spend with patients, the words I speak, drugs I prescribe, some measurable change in the child?

How can this evidence be provided in a satisfactory way? It is clearly impossible, unless the commissioner is broad-minded, Bayesian, and sociologically alert in their interpretation of both evidence and outcome. I would suggest that a commissioner sit in with me for an appointment or two, but even if she were impressed, when she got back to the board-room someone sharper or less trusting than her could point out that I might have only been behaving well because she was in the room and that, no doubt, I sat back and twiddled my thumbs, prescribing dangerously, the moment she had gone. In a less paranoid vein, I wonder if she might doubt that all the effort I was putting in made any difference to the child. Or, even if the child left smiling, what was the difference in five years' time?

I use the term Bayesian in order to suggest that it would be useful if commissioners, in deciding whether or not I am doing my job, brought to the question, not the null hypothesis that I am doing nothing (neither harm, nor good) but a position based on the evidence so far accumulated, which further observation of me may add to incrementally. Unfortunately, I realise as I write, this might work against me, and if it does, it does so in a fascinating parallel with the doctor's own dilemma in treating the individual patient.

The commissioner could come to my clinic with, crudely put, a view that, "Most psychiatrists are doing a good job, so this one probably is too; I shall look for any evidence that sways me either way from this position." Alternatively she might come with the view that, "When clinicians do bad things they are usually acting as individuals. This doctor is an individual (what's more he has emphasised the importance of individuality in his book) so he is likely to do bad things. I shall look for evidence to sway me either way from *this* position."

What this exposes is the risk inherent in my approach. I have elevated the subjective as a source of evidence. The thought experiment with the commissioner shows how evidence and prejudice can become confused. In either scenario she demonstrated a prejudice based on subjectively interpreted evidence. The mental health setting is one in which subjective and objective collide. It is a precious and precarious situation in which patience and an inclusive approach—actually, pretty much everything I argue for here—are required in order to avoid doing violence to it.

The commissioner's assessment of my individual case depends on whether she approaches me as an example of the average doctor, her preconceived notion of a doctor, or the instance of an individual hitherto unknown. The individual clinician has a similar dilemma when confronted with an individual patient. How much do I treat my patient as an example of humanity, an example of a fourteen-year-old male, an example of a fourteen-year-old male with obsessive-compulsive symptoms and a single mother who is a piano teacher, etc. In short, to what extent can I treat my patient as an individual that I am about to learn more about?

It is difficult, therefore, to prove that we are doing any good, if we are to do it properly, rather than pursue someone else's agenda. Daniel

Barenboim (2006), referring to the effect of playing music, describes "a wonderful combination of more knowledge and nothing materially there to show for it". Sometimes the most beneficial effects cannot be demonstrated, and how are we to deliver these to our patients? As outcome measures cannot be reliably defined by the immature and unwell child, there is a danger that they will be defined by others on the child's behalf, instead of co-constructed in the potential space between patient and clinician. This would be the opposite of self-discovery.

The intrusion of stuff

The adult world spreads a great deal of silly *stuff* around the child. Some of the stuff I have already alluded to. I am not talking about the normal developmental realities that a child should be exposed to progressively and at a pace that suits their temperament and ability. I am referring to the complex rules and very serious games that adults play, and sometimes play to the death. Examples might include the fining of parents if their child doesn't get to school, the setting up of complex opt-in arrangements to limit demand on the service, or the fining of the service if it fails to meet a target on the smoking cessation initiative. Adults who display too great a familiarity with this level of reality are often accused of being cynical. The child, a little like the baby being sensitively disillusioned by the good-enough mother, must pay as little attention as possible until they are properly equipped with a sense of self and purpose. The child requires and deserves a degree of protection from this stuff if they are to enjoy the elbow-room necessary for therapeutic development. The psychiatrist paying too much attention to the stuff provides one example of how to *not be with* the child in the clinical setting. Therapeutic *being with* requires a willingness and ability to fend this stuff off, and this requires the taking of risks.

Risk and accountability are two examples of *stuff* that intrudes. There are others, but these are probably the big two.

Containment

In order to be with the child, the clinician must be able to contain any feelings associated with these external pressures. This is not quite the same as abstinence, although abstinence from action can give an impression of containment, however briefly, and the ability to abstain from action is certainly essential for containment to be possible. Containing requires not spilling and, for the sake of efficiency and manageability, requires a degree of effortful encoding of the message or experience. The clinician will not be able to contain all the worries listed above, as well as worries about the safety of their patient, potential for deterioration, side effects of treatment, and the possibility of error on their own part, without a considerable degree of sophisticated internal processing.

Take, for example, worries about the viability of the service that the consultant psychiatrist has fostered and yet which employs him. This relationship, alone, is a Janus-faced and paradoxical one, requiring considerable boggling of internal boundaries. The symbolic child is symbolically parenting its symbolic parent. This analogy works whether one thinks of the clinician as the child or the parent or the service. Therapists, from all angles, attest to the developmental harm caused when an actual child has to make parental adjustments in order to accommodate the uncontained emotions and needs of their actual parents. Here we have, in the normal state of things, an experienced and senior clinician who has developed, cared for, and fostered a service, which effectively exists to support and nourish his activity and development, as well as those of his professional siblings. The parent is parented by the child they parented.

All being well, the people concerned, being adults, are able to behave as adults, and the service behaves as "adult" also. We are all at risk, though, of regressing under pressure. Criticise a service and starve it of resources and it will regress. Its constituent professional components will also resort more and more to their own individual supports, therapies, and needs. Regressed services and regressed professionals are less capable of the mature and sophisticated juggling and alchemy required to keep these pressures away from their relationships with the patient.

If there is a danger of my losing the ability to contain these anxieties (as well as those generated by maintaining the paradoxes and equivocality I have described), and if I am in danger of allowing my regression and the regression of my service to act out in the therapeutic relationship, I need to wonder whether it might be better to abandon the task. After all, first do no harm.

I need to know when I can no longer assume my ability to protect the therapeutic relationship. In order to do so I need to be an expert in *being* and *being with*; I need to know when I am in the room, not simply with my patient plus all they have brought in with them, but also with the commissioners, managers, and my own attendant worries. Being with someone requires me to know with whom, and to limit the numbers. To borrow from my practitioner of the Alexander technique, I can be with others as long as I am with only one or two others.

Summary

- Realities exist in shifting hierarchies and intrude upon each other.
- Some realities are inescapable; others are ungraspable.
- Failing to acknowledge an important reality is one way to lose therapeutic rapport.
- It is important for the therapist to maintain an awareness of and openness to different realities simultaneously and to respond to them deliberately rather than on reflex.
- At times "the way things are" has to be kept at bay so that "the way they might be" can be given a leg-up. Without this, change would be impossible.
- Sometimes, therefore, subjective reality, hopes, and values can be of greater importance than "concrete reality".
- Service delivery is structured according to values. A novel, trending value can displace other values that were embedded, more important, yet under-acknowledged.
- The reconciliation and cooperation of parents can be a metaphor for the integration of apparently irreconcilable values, realities, and polarities. Each is a reality, intruding on the reverie of the other.
- Creativity takes place at the boundary zone between such clashing realities.
- Ultimately, politics intrudes and the clinician has to declare their position. The first priority should be to enable the child in their development towards individuation, agency, and authenticity.
- Behaving as though risk can be abolished is an unhealthy reverie that distorts the clinical encounter.
- The payment by one party for the treatment of another can introduce further distortion as the agenda of change does not arise solely in the potential space between clinician and patient.

CHAPTER THREE

The nature of evidence

E ven a good friend, if they lack the necessary insight, can become a bore and a nuisance if they take too much airtime. This is what has happened, for me, with empirical evidence. I am a scientist by nature and it was a relief when I turned from the study of human laws back to those of science at the end of my first year at university. Yet here I am in the middle of writing a chapter that attempts to put empirical evidence in its place—telling it to shut up for a bit.

I shall try in this chapter to make clear the ways in which I see empirical evidence as having distorted the practice of human and therapeutic relationships, but I shall hope to make it equally clear that it still has a place at the dinner table, provided it sees itself simply as one of the important guests, rather than the only one.

Levels of mistrust

The story of Dr. Harold Shipman (Baker, 2004; Smith, 2002–2005), along with a number of generally less deliberate or sinister healthcare disasters, provides a reminder that dangers lurk and of the need to be wary. Sadly, these stories prompt us particularly to be wary of people who appear caring and kind. Over the last decade or so these reminders have coincided with a burgeoning of the evidence industry, significant societal aversion to risk, and top-down micro-management probably associated with dwindling resources. These things all go together, I suppose. If you can't trust people to be honest or to know themselves (a prerequisite of honesty), then no one can be trusted to make a safe decision on behalf of another, and our caring and treating services need to be cleansed of the personal. Once the market research has been done, the void that was the genuinely personal is filled with anodyne ersatz "personal touch", rather like the prerecorded apology at the railway station, or mass mailings that remember your first name. Given that the genuinely personal is essential to the process of care of all kinds, this becomes an achievement of a pyrrhic nature.

There is something striking about this mistrust. It appears largely to be a mistrust *by* the machinery of society (the organs of government, professional regulation, news media, etc.) *of* the individual, and a mistrust *of* the machinery *by* the individual, examples of the latter being the stories that individuals tell of hospitals, benefit or care arrangements, public transport networks, and suchlike. What seem to arise relatively infrequently are instances of individual patients mistrusting individual health professionals, though it may be that these instances simply don't come to light.

It would be an obvious fallacy to say that, if you can't trust one thing, you should place all your trust in its opposite, and yet something like that seems to be happening. The idea that individuals, perhaps especially from the caring professions, are no longer to be regarded by the machinery of society as trustworthy appears to have resulted in, or at least been accompanied by, an exaggerated faith and reliance on data of the most impersonal kind as an oracle to guide us in all future decisions—the more impersonal, the better. These depersonalised data, stripped of the subjective and the individual, are called "evidence". The word "evidence" has therefore gained both an exaggerated importance and a restricted interpretation.

This does not just apply in the context of healthcare. In the courts, impersonal data have for a long time been referred to as evidence. Fascinatingly, it is a simple oath on a religious text that transforms the dubious personal impressions of individuals into evidence in the court. What seems to have been forgotten is that professionals also swear an oath, or at least adopt a moral code of similar stature and gravitas, which lasts them far longer than a few days in court—typically a lifetime.

When a professional makes a statement of fact or ventures an opinion in the context of their professional work, it is a statement "under oath".

I want to make it clear that I do not object to the empirical, experimental approach in itself. The beauty of a well-designed experiment or mathematical proof is not lost on me any more than the beauty of music, nature, or poetry. There is, I will admit, an emotional and intuitive component to my suspicion of the hegemony of what has become called science (a word derived from the Latin *scire*, to know), but there is a scientific aspect to it as well. I was taught how to read scientific papers, and to uncover their weaknesses. I don't think that I have yet read a paper on treatments in mental health that was free of significant shortcomings, either intrinsic to its conduct or in its application to the real world of clinical care, most particularly in the predictive value of its findings to the next patient I see.

Science: misleading and misled

It is a little as though the scientific method were a young man with Asperger's syndrome creating a stir at a party. I am not sure that is it entirely in its element in the public sphere and influencing policy to the extent that it is doing right now. It has been taken under the wing of some thoroughly disreputable types. The way that it is funded and rewarded creates a series of conflicts of interest such that an unbiased scientist has to take any purported discovery with a pinch of salt. The most pervasive conflict of interest is between our appetites for impact and for honesty. We find, for example, that papers with positive findings are much more likely to be published than those without (Chan & Altman, 2005).

From an etymological perspective, evidence relates to the idea of making visible. We must remember, though, that "seeing is believing" and one should be cautious of the extension of this to the establishment of something as fact. Indeed we probably owe it to ourselves to consider for a moment what we mean by something being a fact. It is very difficult to separate fact from semantics. Whether the object we encounter is a bear or a wolf has at least as much to do with the words "bear" and "wolf" as anything else. And yet we might have a different attitude to basing important decisions on facts on the one hand, and on semantics on the other. Fact-based practice might seem plausible, but semantics-based practice less so.

Furthermore, some kind of issue of the standard of proof seems to have got tangled up in this, possibly though the use of the word in a legal context. In the eyes of the criminal law someone is innocent until proven guilty. This presumption is enshrined in law to reduce the risks of punishing the innocent in a context in which one of two diametrically opposed words—guilty or innocent—is applicable. Transferred out of context, both the either/or dichotomy and the standard of proof may be inappropriate. If something cannot be proven beyond all possible doubt to be true, the conclusion should not be that it is false. If something can be seen, is it there? If it cannot be seen, does that mean that it is not there? In the context of healthcare, the application of this standard of proof is worse than spurious. Individual treatments are placed on trial and then deemed, in relatively general terms, to be either effective or not.

Much empirical evidence has resulted in a reduction in human suffering, but I want us all to be much more alert to the unintended consequences. I am all for evidence, both the signifying word and the thing signified, but I have the following objections to the way that they are being used in the current context:

1. They are interpreted in a way that implies that, if something cannot be proven true, it must be false. This is a fallacy. If something cannot be shown to be helpful, that does not mean that it is not helpful.
2. The above would be a fallacy even within a single context, or when extrapolating between identical contexts. When the contexts differ the conclusion is doubly fallacious. If Janet has no use for a bicycle on a Saturday, this does *not* mean that it will be of no use to John on a Tuesday.
3. The primitive simplification into things being either one thing or its opposite and the utter confusion between being visible, logical, numerical, and being actual, important, reliable, etc. has led to a hopelessly narrow understanding of what constitutes evidence.
4. The exaggerated and exalted position of numbers and of their arcane use, particularly when manipulated at great speed by computers, has led to a dangerous situation where intelligent people take something obscure at face value and believe it—bypassing the scientific understanding that they do possess, as well as their instinct and common sense.

5. All of the above lead us into a reductionist, materialist, primitive
   state of subjugation, and threaten to strip us of the higher qualities
   that make us human and that make life rewarding.

Evidence and "evidence"

In order to make it clear that I am not rejecting both baby and bathwater,
I shall denote as evidence anything that suggests or illustrates the
existence or importance of something. Its absence will not be taken in
any way to be proof that that thing does not exist, or can be ignored.
"Evidence", in quotation marks, will denote the caricature, either/or,
digitalised, over-complicated, addictive, reductive version.

The current and increasing emphasis on "evidence" presents several
problems which I shall expand on:

1. It creates a phobic/obsessive vicious circle.
2. It demeans instinct and teaches us to distrust ourselves.
3. It represents and encourages a lack of trust in others.
4. It has impoverished our notion of the informative.
5. It has drummed placebo out of town.
6. It turns people into countable items.
7. It transmits the virus of utilitarianism.
8. It displaces compassion in the caring professions.
9. It encourages the illusion of certainty.
10. It diminishes the role of hope.

Let me consider these in turn, though we shall find that there is a good
deal of overlap and some repetition.

It creates a phobic, obsessive-compulsive, addictive, vicious circle

Sometimes the selected solution to a problem fuels and increases the
problem, whilst creating an impression that it is still the solution of
choice.

A phobia is an exaggerated fear of something leading to avoidance
of it and reinforced by the temporary relief from anxiety that this avoidance brings. An obsession is an intrusive, repeated, unwanted, and
maladaptive thought. An obsessive compulsion is a difficult-to-resist

urge to carry out a repeated act in order to neutralise the anxiety caused by an obsessive thought. It is easy to see how these concepts can be applied to the process I have described above. One can think of these phenomena in, for example, cognitive-behavioural or more Freudian terms. In the former, one would place emphasis on the relationship between more or less conscious thoughts, behaviours, and emotional and bodily experience, linked in a behavioural cycle. In the latter, one might be more interested in the role of unconscious and arguably more fundamental anxieties. In either model I would suggest that violation and catastrophic loss are prominent objects of avoidance.

Our relentless and stereotyped (compulsive) search for reassurance in the form of "evidence" is the behaviour that temporarily assuages our fear at a superficial level, but in such a way that the search is immediately resumed. The call, at the end of each published research paper, for further research on the topic is reminiscent of the front-door obsessive who turns back for one last check to be sure, and then a further one to be even surer. Or the arachnophobe who, having vacuumed the room for a fourth time that day, decides to introduce the further measure of taping up all the skirting boards.

There is no pharmacological solution to the societal version of the problem, and psychodynamic approaches would require a degree of therapeutic commitment that it would be impossible to establish on a societal scale, though psychodynamic insights could influence policy. It should be possible, however, to follow an effectively cognitive-behavioural approach to the problem, even on a societal scale. The treatment involves exposure and response—prevention. We don't need to work too hard on the exposure part of it; there is a ready supply of threat. It might be the threat of pain, loss of life, dignity, autonomy, loved-ones, or the uncertainty of the afterlife. Whatever it is, we are already amply exposed to it. The treatment involves preventing our compulsive response. We need to remove the element of compulsion. When the paper concludes "Further research is required …" we need to be able to say, "… or perhaps not", and then carry out the organisational equivalent of a relaxation exercise.

This is where the addiction model may assist. We may be able to achieve a degree of safe and moderate indulgence in the behaviour, though in the clinical context experience shows that this is particularly difficult. I am in no doubt that there is great value in empirical scientific evidence, so I very much hope that we can achieve a use for it without doing so exclusively and compulsively. I hope we can continue to use it in moderation and do not require the rigidity of going cold turkey, but it may be that the very aggressive behaviours of some societal groups represent a counter-rigidity of that kind.

I have so far focused mainly on the obsessive aspect of this analogy. There is an aspect of phobia that may shed further light on the process that I am trying to evidence: the hypervigilance to threat that is found in phobia. The arachnophobe is extremely sensitive and alert to circumstances or signs that suggest the possible presence of spiders. As the poet Adrian Mitchell put it, "For a man who hated reptiles so obsessively/He spend an awful lot of time in their company." (Mitchell, 1982, p. 142). Poetic sense dictated the use of the word obsessively where clinical sensibilities might have dictated a word better associated with phobia. The point, though, is made. We fear pain and loss so much that we spend much of our time thinking about it.

How are we to get to know ourselves, other than by making up our own minds and making mistakes? We cannot feel without exposure to pain, love without the threat of loss. The more we rely on so-called objective information, the less we shall have the experience of doing these things that, together, amount to living. We shall not grow or reach maturity without exposure to risk and the consequences of our own choices, and we are not taking proper responsibility for our choices if the evidence is summed up for us into a dichotomous presence or absence of a seal of approval.

By avoiding these objects of our phobic attention, we reinforce our belief that it is essential to go on doing so. There are thresholds we dare not cross for fear that a risk may be lurking on the other side. We repeatedly wash our hands in statistics, these being a cerebral equivalent of the germicidal hand-pumped gel.

If we are averse to risk, addicted to perfection, and hypervigilant in our gathering of information, we shall become extremely good at collecting evidence of failure liable to perpetuate our fears. We may even inadvertently steer situations such that our phobic beliefs are confirmed and our addiction fed.

It demeans instinct and teaches us to distrust ourselves

Because "evidence" is perceived to have integrity and worth, each of which is apparently vulnerable to corrosive contamination by the subjective, our reliance on it leads us to distrust our own senses, thoughts, and feelings. This is a shame, as they are actually the only evidence that each of us has to go on. However this "evidence" is concocted or come by, it reaches us through our senses, and is evaluated by our thoughts and feelings.

We are confused about what is trustworthy. Consider the advice we give to children. We tell them, for example, of "stranger danger": do not accept sweets or lifts from strangers. Then it is pointed out to us that most abuse is carried out by someone known to the child. How to advise the child now? The answer, of course, should be to teach the child to read the signs themselves. No one knows exactly what the signs are or how a child would come by the information, and so the wisest advice has probably been "trust your instincts". This was the message behind the "good touch—bad touch" that emerged a few years ago. Attempts to formalise this by explaining to children that touching in a certain area of the body is wrong seemed like good sense until we realised that, first, the child's GP might need to do this in order to provide appropriate care and, second, a sexual predator is unlikely to start their advance by touching within the "swimsuit area". We are vulnerable to those we trust and to whom we are beholden: "He was nice to me before and I owe him for the mobile phone." We are probably better to do what we can to provide our children with what they really need (not electronic gadgets but food, warmth, love, and respect), and then encourage them to trust their instincts whilst gradually removing the scaffolding of our direct observation of them.

It is immediately apparent that adults are increasingly discouraged from applying this rule in their own lives. Whether or not something seems right to us, we should await the "evidence" to tell us how to feel and what to think about it, as though our initial feelings and thoughts don't themselves amount to evidence. We are groomed by experts who help us to invest our money and then tell us what to buy with it.

When I say that "evidence" "demeans instinct", it is with considerable bitterness. I experience a confusing irritation when I encounter findings from functional magnetic resonance imaging (fMRI) research that the same part of the brain "lights up" whether the subject is experiencing emotional pain or physical pain (Kross, Berman, Mischel, Smith & Wager, 2011). It is, of course, exciting, but I have known this for a long time. We have *all* known it for a long time! How come? Well, the clue was in the word "pain". We could be erudite about this and consider other languages, past and foreign—the French *douleur*, Shakespearian *dolor*, etc.—but even in current common parlance it is blindingly obvious. No one hearing a woman talking about an ex-partner who has caused her "so much pain over the years" would think she was talking about physical pain, though there may have been that also. And it would be a sign of limited pragmatic language skills if one person fluent in idiomatic English, accused by another of being a "pain in the neck", were to protest that they hadn't touched the person's neck.

We have known this for a long time because our language revealed it to us. As Winnicott said, "if what I say has truth in it, this will already have been dealt with by the world's poets," (1986, p. 173). He went on to say that the painstaking work of science is also necessary, but the point is that the poets got there first. "Evidence" is in the slow lane, and we should feel demeaned when we are rather condescendingly told that we may have been right all along.

And why would anyone bother about my being annoyed by this? These clinicians are, themselves, a bit of a pain, whinging on about their feelings! The fact of the matter is that if my patient is to obtain benefit from the link between physical and emotional pain then it is better if this is something that is "discovered" in the course of the clinical encounter. No doubt someone will be able to prove this also using fMRI, in due course, but we know it is true. People are more open to ideas that they have come across or developed themselves. My clinical practice should support this therapeutic process of discovery that provides freedom from symptoms (of addiction, as above) and boosts self-esteem. I do not pretend ignorance of the connection, but I retain and expose a genuine reticence about the knowledge and I wonder if it might apply in each patient's case. The point is that my uncertainty and wondering are not the result of ignorance, but of experience and (dare I say it?) wisdom. So the scientific findings, their bumptious confidence, and the emphasis that is placed on them, insult my own scientific knowledge, wisdom, experience, and art, and insult my patient's discovery of the link in himself, thereby undermining its therapeutic power.

I said that "evidence" is in the slow lane. I acknowledge that life may be at less risk in the slow lane. In the clinical encounter we have a slow lane of our own. It is sensitive to the traffic conditions in that person, that family, on that day, and when the conditions allow us to do so safely, you will not see us for dust. The acceleration possible in the clinical situation is phenomenal. To stretch the analogy a little too far: consider the juggernaut deriding the Ferrari for its lack of engineering finesse. Let me be quite clear. The vast lumbering industry of "evidence" is *not* the Ferrari. The Ferrari is aesthetically designed, phenomenally powerful, and requires experience behind the wheel.

It represents and encourages a lack of trust in others

The "evidence" movement has taught us not only that our own instincts are not to be trusted, but also that we should only trust what someone else says if they have followed a prescribed formula. And if they have followed the formula we are inclined to trust them blindly, or against our better judgement.

Evidently, life is to be lived along the lines of the childhood game Simon Says (a game which, interestingly, is typically played between one adult and a group of children). In this game you take instructions and act on them but, to avoid elimination, you only do so if the instruction is prefixed with the formula "Simon Says". Games are there to teach us how to cope with problems in life. They should not be played for real. One person tells another what to do, but to forestall their objection or non-compliance, she dresses the instruction up as something that has been handed down to her. The rules of Simon Says are strikingly similar to those of "evidence" in which any statement I make is taken seriously only if I refer to the fact that someone else said it before I did. It is a way of making an utterance seem more objective. It is not I who am instructing, but the facts, the evidence, the protocol, the policy, etc.

A few pages ago I wrote, "In order to be with the child, the psychiatrist must be able to contain any feelings associated with these external pressures". I could have written, "In order to be with the child, the psychiatrist must be able to contain[23, 24] any feelings associated with these external pressures.[25, 26,27]" Would you have been more convinced? The danger is that you might have been, even without turning to the back and checking that the numbers were repeated next to plausible references. My impression is that most people don't properly chase up references and I could quite possibly get away with inventing a few. It is interesting how close perfectly acceptable academic writing can come to a sophisticated form of plagiarism.

I am denying neither the importance of consensus and conflict in scientific research and discovery nor the expedience of one generation of scientists standing on the shoulders of their predecessors. I am concerned at the effect that a blinkered adherence to this practice can have on the human experience, particularly if its values, assumptions and rules are allowed to escape unnoticed from their proper place. Again, it is the unintended consequences I want to draw out into the light.

My concern is that this practice of justifying opinion on the basis of other opinions is, first, that it may represent an instance of "group-think" (Janis, 1971) and, second, that utterances will be taken at face value if they are encumbered by these trappings of science (complex explanation, obscure methods, multiple nested references, etc.) rather than the reader testing them against her own experience and understanding.

So much for the erosive effect that the Simon Says approach can have on people's trust in themselves (or in anyone other than Simon). Further erosion stems from our fear of culpability in a blaming, litigious culture. It is evident how reluctant we are to accept that things can go wrong without a person being held to account. Weather forecasters are blamed for the damage caused by hurricanes. Transgression, negligence, and ignorance can of course have a role to play and the importance of identifying these and enabling their reduction should not be denied. An attempt to encourage the errant to come forward—or perhaps to prevent a panicked brain-drain out of the professions—has led to the notion of a "no blame culture". Yet the cynical impression seems to be prevalent, that the so-called no blame culture actually hunts down, exposes, and scapegoats at least as much as did its predecessor. So, in order to sidestep the blame when something goes wrong (which it will) one pre-emptively constructs a defence along the lines of, "Simon told me to sir." The guidelines tell me to refer an anxious child for cognitive behavioural therapy. But it *feels* wrong to me to put a ten-year-old child on a one-year waiting list for an eight-session course of cognitive behavioural therapy (CBT). That is what the guidelines encourage me to do, rather than to meet with them and their parents, understand their predicament, and offer them a powerful companion, albeit a busy one. My defence, if I neglected my instincts (and the child) would be, "I was following orders," and this rings a chilling bell.

Allied to the no blame culture is the notion of transparency, which sounds nice. Transparent is good while obscure is bad. Why? Translucency, not transparency, is what is required for a bathroom window, and sometimes total obscuring is necessary. Some things only grow in the dark. I would like to explore this idea of transparency a little and I shall do so by taking it back to the primary dyad.

A parent, when asked by a young child, "When will you be back?" does not say, "I hope to be back at six, in time for tea but, as I am driving, there is a likelihood I shall be held up by traffic, and a small possibility that I shall be killed in a car crash." The parent says, "I shall see you at six sweetheart."

The child probably colludes with this evasion, to an extent. Children tend not to hear the things that they cannot bear as long as the parent manages to hide his own fear. The arrangement is as follows. The child asks a question. The parent gives a confident and reassuring answer that bears a reasonable approximation to the truth, this enabling him to deliver it with congruent affect. The child accepts it. The world is fine. Hopefully the other parent doesn't expose the healing lie. Perhaps much later they all own up.

The problem is that the parent, and any person or organisation in an analogous role, has to be able to hide some things. It is unlikely that humans could support the full weight of knowing everything. We fall from paradise if we eat too much of the fruit of the tree of knowledge. We probably need government agencies to gather information and to keep the fact secret. I am not sure if I would want to know the real motivation for the war I was to give my life to. I would prefer a version of the truth that enabled me to continue with positive morale. What we need is to be able to trust the other—the person or the organisation in power—enough to be able to get on with things. Total distrust paralyses.

The trouble with genuine transparency is that it is can be unhelpful for the reasons given above. Furthermore, insistence on the importance of transparency teaches us to be distrustful of anything that is not "transparent" when there might be very good reasons for opacity. At the same time, because transparency has gained such leverage in obtaining trust and credibility, there is a risk that organisations will devise ways to disguise concealment (which they know is necessary) as transparency (which they believe is required). It calls to mind the conjuror that makes a great show of getting you to check that there is nothing up his sleeve whilst he slips the ace into your own top pocket. Take the minutes of committee meetings: openly available, desperately tedious, meticulously recording absences, apologies, and action points, whilst the truly important decisions are made before and after the meeting in private conversations between a select few. What organs of power say no longer has the ring of truth and there is a cycle of distrust breeding further incongruent protestations of benign intention and "transparency". Rhetoric so often appears to be a tool that large organisations use when they want to disguise one thing as its opposite.

The redemption to be glimpsed within this rather paranoid construction lies in the ability of ordinary people to see through the charade, make jokes about committees, and then rather wisely carry on with their lives, regardless.

It will be evident from the above that, a) I believe that we need to be able to trust and, if nothing else, to trust in our instincts, b) we need to be able to be lied to. There is no easy or painless way out of this double bind.

Milan Kundera defines kitsch as the denial of the existence of shit and alerts us to the possible relationship between totalitarianism and the denial of "shit" (1984, p. 248). A widening gap between rhetoric and reality should be a sinister sign in a society's development. Of course, objective inquiry through scientific method can be one of the most important weapons against this slide into corruption, but even scientists—perhaps especially scientists because of their necessarily narrow focus and their temperamental naivety—can prove blind to the subtle misuse of their efforts. Even if they are alert to the potential misuse of the explicit fruits of their labours—the statements that they generate—the risk remains that they are not sufficiently alert to, or interested in, the covert messages that their methods and language endorse.

So the teaching that we must not trust our instincts, leads to our not trusting our caregivers. Then we demand of them the complete truth (like a child who has glimpsed or been shown the flaws in the healing lie). The complete and honest truth is unbearable, or is deemed unpalatable, so a more elaborate lie is told, accompanied by florid protestations as to the essential value of "transparency". The whole structure becomes corrupt and we become frenetically addicted to information. We demand the faster and more fulsome production of information, therefore requiring an industrial process of production. Like any industrial process, this one creates a number of more or less invisible by-products, many of which are corrosive.

It has impoverished our notion of the informative

Since we can no longer trust any information that is merely spoken by a human, we demand a special category of information. It must be produced in industrial quantities, as above, and it is given a trustworthy name, chosen by its associations (a study of positive risk in middle adolescence might be called PRIMAx). It is called "evidence". It must not be produced by a simple process, but by an impressive and, if possible, arcane one. It must not grow on trees.

When there is an inordinate demand for a specific commodity, there tends to be a rush towards a monopoly on its production. There is no injustice in the empirical method winning this race. Its credentials are good. But observe how it has become distorted by the development of distrust: a couple of hundred years ago an august and well-funded gentleman (*sic*) could go to another country and draw what he saw there. This was evidence. In the same way, a psychiatrist might describe the transformation in his patient. If he was august enough (and possibly well funded) he might be believed. But what if he had concocted a lie in order to be published more widely and gain further recognition and the funds for a further exploration or a bigger clinic? This has probably happened. We are not content to oust this individual, we become determined to oust him *and all his like*. We do not simply keep a closer eye on him, but also on all people involved in similar ventures. We demand to see their measuring devices and contemporaneous notes. We want them to have done a fair test.

So far, so good, but we go further; we do not want the encouraging results of this work to be due to personal qualities because these cannot easily be transferred and so cannot become a commodity. We therefore demand methods that eliminate personal and subjective qualities. Notice at this point the over-determined quality of the argument, how the reasons for, and the means of, eliminating the subjective proliferate and overlap.

The experimenter is required to have "blinded" herself and her subjects so that the power of persuasion could not be blamed for the outcome. Of course, persuasion might have been an important part of the treatment but we did not want persuasion and its connotations of being tricked to be part of the process of convincing us—the reader of the research—and so we want it eliminated from the treatment also.

Then the experiment must be repeated, in case it was a one-off. More and more elaborate ways are devised to count the results, weigh them against each other, and eliminate the personal. Preferably they should be so complex that a computer is needed. In this way we can reassure ourselves that we are in the hands of a machine, rather than a human with their confounded common sense, dreams, and fears. In order to eliminate human error we have eliminated the human.

There is a serious problem: the people making and selling the product are the very ones developing the methods put in place to reassure us of the incorruptibility of it. It is a little like the pop-up message on your computer that tells you: "Your system may have been infiltrated, so buy this cleansing software." They develop the commodity. They develop the method of encryption. They sell us their expertise in decryption. They explain all of this to us (we barely understand) and thereby we are reassured that we are not being cheated.

I am fairly certain that this is not done intentionally. I have played my own small part in the process, and I certainly did not do so with any cynical intent. I suspect that it is due to inherent human frailty, a result of our individual unconscious and subconscious drives enacted in a complex structure called society. But we have become like the nations that eradicate the rainforest in order to grow more palm oil, blind to the fact that the funeral pyre included such treasures as reason, experience, analogy, instinct, and memory. Some of the richest sources of evidence are in danger of extinction, while we breathe the toxic products of their combustion.

It has drummed placebo out of town

In that smouldering debris would also be found suggestion, persuasion, and hope. If we could revive them they would provide our healing with a precious boost.

That part of a treatment effect that cannot be attributable to specific and transferable components (transferable from one clinician to another as well as from one patient to another) is called the placebo effect. Indeed, some of the effects that are transferable, such as the colour and size of a tablet, have been found to be part of, or to influence, the placebo effect (Evans, 1985, p. 216; Thompson, 2005, p. 41). There is a science of the placebo effect. As a defender of placebo I should probably be delighted in this, but I am worried that the magic will be eradicated in the process of its dissection. In its efforts to establish the mechanism inherent in the transferable part of the treatment—the pill or the therapeutic technique—the "evidence" industry has had to split off those aspects of the treatment that belong to the persons of the clinician and patient, and the relationship between them. (A fact, incidentally, that places those therapies that explicitly use this relationship at a distinct disadvantage when it comes to justifying their ongoing existence.)

I was in conversation with a general practitioner a year or so ago about placebo. It is often in the full flow of an earnest conversation that implied meanings and values slip out. I am confident that she is someone who would never make a distinction between pain and "real pain", particularly in front of the patient, yet she used the phrase "real analgesic effect" as though a distinction could be made between the analgesic effect of a placebo and the analgesic effect of a "real analgesic". What distinguishes these two would not be the subjective effect. They might be distinguishable in terms of some of their physiological effects although it will now emerge that placebo produces neurophysiological effects that correlate with their analgesic effects. The main distinction between these preparations is the intent ascribed either to their manufacture or to their prescription. One is intended to be an analgesic and the other a placebo. Surely, if paracetamol produces no pain relief, whereas taking a "placebo" is followed by a reduction in perceived pain (irrespective of whether there are accompanying physiological changes), it is the latter that has the "real analgesic effect".

The paradox in this situation should be obvious. It seems that a painkiller has to be something that we have manufactured and that can be packaged and sold. In short, a marketable commodity. It does not matter whether or not it relieves pain in a given individual because in trials it has been shown that it can do so *on average* (see below). Indeed, if it does not work in a given individual, the stigma appears to be attached to the individual, rather than to the drug: "This is a painkiller, so there is something wrong with you if your pain is not relieved by it."

A further paradox attaches to the fact that all the effort that goes into stripping the placebo effect from a treatment probably actually enhances the placebo effect. That is to say that, if the doctor has attended faraway conferences given by famous scientists with foreign accents, and if she has read complex articles with a lot of arcane process, and if she knows that the "evidence" supports the use of a particular treatment (which is marketed under a name that sounds scientific but also includes phonemes reminiscent of words like "ability", "effective", "certain"), and that the national regulatory bodies have endorsed this treatment, then she is likely to believe in it, and to convey this belief to the patient. In short, all of these things are likely to boost the placebo effect of the drug. Perhaps the industry has managed to commodify the placebo effect after all—but notice that it is the expensive (and relatively dangerous) placebo that we are encouraged to use, fuelling the industry and externalising our locus of control.

How does *being with* apply in this situation? When I contemplate myself in the room with someone presenting with what are now grandiosely called "medically unexplained symptoms" (grandiose on the part of medicine because it implies that medicine should be able to explain everything and anything it cannot explain falls somehow into a special category), I find myself relegating this narrow notion of "evidence" while I spend time with my patient. "I am with my patient now. Please leave us alone for the moment." What emerges is another kind of knowledge. I know that this person is in pain and that he has come to me for help. I know that it will not be helpful to tell him that his pain is not real. I have some inkling, perhaps from instinct, perhaps from experience, that it may not help him to be told that there is no medical explanation for his pain. What I tend to do, I think, is to talk about the experience that has been called "pain" and the surrounding context and contingencies, until we reach the point where we can acknowledge that what medical doctors think or do in relation to this person's pain has so far not been helping him, other than by making medical inaction safe (by ruling out dangerous treatable illness). I listen to him for signs of what may have helped in the past or may help in the future. I even open my mind to the possibility that it may not be in his greater interests to be free of this particular symptom. I adopt a less judgemental (and more mindful) position. It is a little like motivational interviewing; the new ideas (therapeutic ideas) have to be discovered, rather than pushed into the conversation. I think that *being with* has a role to play here—being with the patient and relegating assumptions and my own need for reassurance.

Before leaving "medically unexplained symptoms" I shall return our attention to this expectation that medicine can explain everything, an expectation so strong that we seem to regard as slightly suspect, anything that frustrates it. Medically unexplained symptoms are simply symptoms that have not (yet) been explained or removed by medical science. In the same way a placebo effect is a treatment effect that has not been explained (or intended) by medical science. Each is stigmatised, presumably on the basis that it is abnormal and undesirable for anything to be inexplicable or to frustrate our intentions in this way.

Placebo response is highly variable, sometimes influenced by surprising factors, but a frequent finding is of relatively high placebo response rates in children and adolescents (Weimer et al., 2013). All of this could be and is being studied, but there are a couple of issues to draw out here. One is that the placebo response rate is so often regarded as a problem. Clearly it is a problem for the drug companies trying to produce research to justify the use of medications. It is less clear why it should be seen as a problem from the clinical perspective. It seems to me that a high placebo response rate could be regarded as evidence of a greater ability in the patient to recover from setbacks, master her experience, and move on.

I remember in training when we were presented with a paper on the treatment of depression in adolescents that showed the response rate to antidepressants to be no greater than to placebo. What I experienced was a sense of being disarmed. A therapeutic option had been taken away from me. We went on prescribing. If asked, I suppose we would have justified this by identifying some shortcomings of the paper (there are always a few). What bothered me was not so much the fact that the antidepressant might effectively be acting as a placebo, as the implication that I should no longer prescribe this fairly effective treatment on the grounds that it had been "outed".

We have a problem with the idea of deliberately using placebo for the purposes of treatment. It is easy to see why. The trust necessary in a relationship between patient and doctor makes the idea of an actively deceitful doctor particularly repellant. We could be more adventurous, though. First, a much quoted though uncontrolled study suggests that the effect of a placebo may not be entirely lost when it is unmasked (Park & Covi, 1965). Second, the ethics and legality of parents consenting on behalf of their children raises the enticing possibility of ethically prescribing a placebo to a child with therapeutic purpose.

A large number of general practitioners (GPs) have said that they have used placebo (Howick et al., 2013), but others in the profession find it an objectionable practice. Society and the professions have in recent decades developed some very reasonable concerns about paternalism, and yet in the clinical relationship the professional must hold something back. If we become totally neutral and transmit unfiltered all the factual information to hand—an impracticable position, of course, given the quantity of information and the uncertainty of its accuracy and applicability—we would be doing our patients a great disservice. We have to be selective in the information we deliver and so a degree of paternalism is inevitable. Is there a moral difference between prescribing an antidepressant, privately believing that its main modus would be via the placebo effect, and prescribing a placebo, privately believing the same? Their chances of proving beneficial may be roughly comparable, and it is the marketed treatment that is likely to carry greater physiological risk to the patient. I can see here a moral argument in favour of the use of placebo.

It turns people into countable units

Because we need a machine to absolve our oracle from the sins of human motivation and error, we require binary elements for it to count and stack. Studies are performed on humans reduced to their countable attributes—preferably a small number of attributes *or* a very large number of humans.

Actually, for each patient I am about to treat, I would like the study that was carried out prospectively with a long follow-up (but using today's treatments) on a few people *exactly* like my patient. As this is impossible, humans who still have their humanity intact must be herded together in such a way that it can be ignored: neutered by their number.

It is not only the individual research subjects of these studies who are reduced to countable units, but the patients are too. On the one hand, diagnosis, in its most crudely categorical form, reduces patients to examples of the entities studied in the clinical trials. At the same time they become countable units as evidence that the clinicians are working. They become "patient contacts" or "assessments", "treatment episodes", and "discharges". Of course, one cannot count everything—every greeting, every time I say "Can you manage these steps?", every explanation I give or open question I ask. They are collected on a flavour of the month basis. This year it may be the number of weeks from referral to the onset of treatment (as though this should be a standard for everyone, and as though it were possible to identify at what point treatment has started or stopped in mental health services). Next week it might be whether or not I follow up patients every month for the next three months after initiating a prescription (as though that made more sense or was safer than a telephone call after two weeks, and appointments spaced according to the nature of the prescription and the patient's response). These are real examples.

People are averaged, reduced, and counted. They become an example of something. I ignore the fact that my patient's grandfather was a pipe-smoker because that information does not help in the classification process. Individuality becomes an anomaly because the individual characteristics (as opposed to the characteristics of the clinical entities) are either inconvenient or ignored obstacles to the research or treatment protocol.

I suspect that the intuition of the clinician derives from the subtle, near miraculous, complex, bordering-on-chaotic, cerebral computation of a vast number of observations ranging from the obvious, taught at clinical school, through to subliminal gestures and features. The clinician is no longer encouraged to pay attention to the intuitive sense that a certain intervention is likely to benefit the particular patient sat before her on a particular occasion. Instead she has to turn to the off-the-peg, impersonal, quite possibly manualised, treatment provided.

I want to keep remembering that the empirical evidence can be useful whilst at the same time repeatedly drawing attention to perverse outcomes. It is not just the *being with* that suffers, but also the "hard" clinical practice. The clinician operating in a bald empirical paradigm is expected to imagine the patient sitting before her as one of a faceless, characterless herd: this is a patient with depression; therefore she needs cognitive behavioural therapy or possibly cognitive behavioural therapy plus a selective serotonin reuptake inhibitor. But what if she is also suffering from hypothyroidism, or has an IQ of 180 and doesn't like being told by someone a third of her age to think differently? What if she has a sub-clinical smidgen of autism, or has tried CBT before? What if she is being abused and hasn't told anyone yet?

The fact that money is short and the publicly funded clinician is a public good requires the collection of another category of evidence that demonstrates that we are doing the right thing. Whether these data are required by commissioning groups, or are of interest to me, they amount once more to the reduction of people to numbers and instances of this condition or that practice.

The psychologist Liam Hudson put it well in *The Cult of the Fact* when he said, "To know about ... people, in a way that reduces them to thing-hood, is to pursue knowledge in a way that is inimical to the proper growth of human self-awareness" (Hudson, 1972, p. 76).

It transmits the virus of utilitarianism

When you have been trained into reducing your patient to a category of disorder, and carrying out your job as though you were on steel rails, regarding it as done if the score on a questionnaire has dropped below a predetermined threshold, then you have allowed a Trojan horse into your practice and it has spilled its contents.

These contents are many. The application of "evidence" and the routine utilisation of outcome measures implant a number of implied values and then, like a stage hypnotist, erase from memory all trace of their insertion. By relying on and rehearsing certain assumptions, we promote and promulgate them. For example, assumptions that one person with depression is like another person with depression, that the principal complaint is the thing that needs to be changed, that if something is of value then it can be measured (or that *value* can be measured), that relationship may be reduced to a process of information exchange, or that a person's predicament can be adequately represented by symptom scores. So a side effect of "evidence" is the reinforcement of fallacies and the promotion of certain values.

One of the things smuggled in by virtue of being taken for granted is the utilitarian ethic. There is a large number of outcome measures and relatively few process measures. Furthermore, the former are regarded as the more important. If we are bound to practise according to "evidence" as defined above, we must have a measurable outcome as our goal, rather than subjective impressions of patient, parent, or clinician. Indeed, thanks to the topical "payment by results" approach I have seen, in print, "stable housing" as an outcome for a mental health intervention. This is plainly absurd. The provision of affordable housing is not in the sphere of control of the mental health service. Stable and affordable housing serves mental health more than the reverse.

The end needs to be defined by counting, and then the chosen end justifies the means. The means adopted should help to inform us as to which sorts of endings to take seriously, but the opposite seems to apply. The value of trying to help is eclipsed by an overemphasis on the apparently objective criterion of whether or not one is actually helping. An action is carried out because of its measurable utility (to someone else) rather than because it is virtuous, enjoyed, or appreciated in its own right.

There is something intrinsically unappealing about success. It is the trying that attracts us. Novels and sporting events draw out the trying as long as possible. When we do celebrate the success, the exuberance of the celebration is proportional to the effort that went into the achievement. We do not give gold medals to the tallest athlete or the one with the most expensive bicycle. Success without genuine effort seems rather ruthless and cold: thank you and good night. We need to redefine the aim of treatment. Not simply a score that triggers a separation and that signifies getting rid, but something that acknowledges the value of the shared journey.

It displaces compassion

By regarding clinicians and patients as assets and treatment episodes, respectively, and by inadvertently valuing categorical outcomes over process and discovery—the attainment of a score over the mutual reward of existence and companionship—this very narrow form of evidence and the consequent rendering of humans into countable units risks the marginalisation of compassion.

> Four children were playing in a rough patch of land beyond the school playing fields when one of them slipped and fell, twisting his ankle so that he could no longer walk or stand. He subsided in pain. Two of the group ran to the school buildings to fetch a member of staff. The fourth stayed with the injured boy, one hand touching his back, and looked with consternation, alternately at his face, the ankle, and in the direction of the school. Anxiously he asked, "Are you all right?"

Compassion can be aroused in, and is no less valuable coming from, the relatively powerless. What is more, there is a particular levelling quality to being with someone that you are powerless to help and compassion in this situation can be reciprocal and redeeming. Perhaps as a consequence, compassion has been misunderstood as a soft and ineffectual thing. But powerlessness is not necessary for compassion. Compassion can be—and indeed needs to be—present in the relationship between a powerful helper and a vulnerable person. And, if one is going to intervene—to *do* something—it is important to have a good idea of the likely effects of intended action. Empirically derived evidence may be important at this point.

Measuring and counting are essential for the derivation of empirical information. They will miss and therefore under-prescribe the intangible and subjective, though, and their role in summarising the achievement of a mental health team is highly questionable.

An emphasis on material (quantifiable) outcomes encourages us to rush *to do* the thing that "works" or can be measured and has face validity. There is a problem with both the choice of action, therefore, as well as the rushing. When faced with pain, loss, and fear, it can be tremendously comforting to have something *to do about it*, but this is not the same as offering compassion. And receiving compassion is not *being done to*. If I understand correctly, those members of staff in Mid Staffordshire who "metaphorically walked on the other side of the ward" (Francis, 2013, p. 1015) had jobs to do and targets of their own to meet.

Whether the determination to act to reduce suffering is considered part of compassion or part of the duty of care, what is required is the discernment to know when to act directly and for the individual, and when to continue to be a cog in the machine.

Wanting to help and helping are not the same, and each has value. The utilitarian emphasis draws our attention more and more to the action linked to the measurable outcome and away from the patient's experience and intangible need. The more the measurable and organisational agenda is emphasised, the less is the action likely to flow from compassion for the patient (or the colleague who is being bullied). Compassion by its very nature is more closely allied to personal, as opposed to the corporate or population-based, needs and it is uniquely placed to respond to the intangible and subjective.

Whether compassion is *antecedent* to action or synchronous with it, the compassion, impulse, and action are distinct. "I want to help" is desire, "doing this may help" is either hope or empiricism. The actual doing of it is action, and is at times best done dispassionately. The person who croons "I *so* want to help" as he dresses the wound is not being compassionate; he is being self-indulgent and irritating. He should be *with* the patient as he carries out the action, and compassion for the person he is with will drive *how* he acts.

Displacement of compassion will be corporately denied. The rhetoric will require compassion and will thereby undermine it, since the action will be motivated by the requirement rather than the impulse.

It is not only the compassion of doctor for patient that matters, but also vice versa. Mutual compassion is about being human and healthy. I cannot feel compassion for a unit of sickness, and it may be hard for many to feel compassion for a person who refuses to be turned into a unit of sickness and therefore threatens the necessary digital returns. The patient may also be less likely to feel compassion for, and pleasure in the relationship with, someone who is treating her in this way.

Being with is, by definition, a compassionate stance. Our attention should be first and foremost towards the patient and her predicament, with an open mind to what the relationship will reveal and require. When intervention is called for, the clinician should reach behind them for the evidence, rather as a surgeon puts a hand out for the artery clamp.

It encourages the illusion of certainty

There is less in the way of certainty in this world than most of us would like. We are forever checking weather forecasts and taking out insurance policies. By making proclamations and predictions within narrow confidence-limits and about elements abstracted from reality, "evidence" convinces us that certainty can be achieved, feeds our addiction to the notion, and paradoxically ends up telling us very little about the real world that faces us.

Evidence, in its broader sense, is something that shows or illuminates. It enables something to be seen, even if what is revealed is no more than a possibility. It is to be distinguished from "evidence", that product and fuel of a fear-driven pursuit of the illusion of certainty. Certainty is the ever-elusive holy grail of the obsessionally anxious. In the following chapter I shall describe the therapeutic value of uncertainty. I shall do this despite the fact that certainty, albeit illusory, has its uses; it just doesn't need any encouragement.

It diminishes the role of hope

I cannot prove that this antidepressant or this course of cognitive behavioural therapy will successfully cure this patient's depression, even if *post hoc* the person gets better I do not have proof of causation. Why then do I prescribe these things? All I have to go on is information on probability—and hope. The research may be useful insofar as it makes my hope a reasonable one, but it is hope, not certainty, that drives me to encourage my patient into taking time, effort, and a potentially unpleasant or dangerous drug. If I waited for a standard of proof "beyond all possible doubt" before embarking on a clinical action I would never do anything. Yet when I present my assertion to the boardroom I am expected to provide a supporting argument that places it exactly there—beyond all possible doubt. The boardroom is unlikely to fund my project on the strength of my hope.

This application of completely different standards to how the clinician is managed and how the clinician manages her patient requires the diligent clinician to hold within herself a San Andreas Fault, waiting for catastrophe. This, too, can best be managed by the judicious application of hope.

Summary

- Human frailty and intolerance of risk have taught us to distrust the personal and to place our faith in the impersonal and mechanical.
- The notion of what constitutes "evidence" has become increasingly simplistic and the process by which it is obtained, increasingly arcane.
- Empirical science is abused by powerful interests and is easily misunderstood by the public.
- The tripartite process of purchasing, providing, and receiving healthcare results in the use of measurable outcomes to evaluate service provision.
- An overemphasis on this dichotomous, narrow, mechanistic, brand of evidence can be seen to have a number of undesirable effects in healthcare including:
  - the fuelling of the phobic/obsessional relationship with an elusive and illusory certainty;
  - the marginalisation of instinct, trust, compassion, and hope;
  - the rendering of people into countable units, commodifying interpersonal relationships and infiltrating them with a utilitarian ethic;
  - the impoverishment of our notion of both evidence and treatment.
- Provided we allow ourselves continuity of contact with our patient over time, we may be able to inform and refine our decisions in their care through an iterative process of relatively direct observation and qualitative feedback.

- *Being with* the patient involves the use micro-iterations, remaining receptive to our internal cues as well as to conscious and subliminal feedback from our patient on a moment-to-moment basis and evolving throughout the course of their treatment.
- This amounts to the sensitive gathering and use of a kind of evidence that is rich, personalised, and lacking in dangerous side effects.

CHAPTER FOUR

Uncertainty, the mother (or father) of hope

Richard Holloway, referring to a raging religious debate, described the noise of clashing opinion as "the thickest of over-coats to cover us against the chill of uncertainty" (2012, p. 196). Holloway's memoir is a study of the importance of uncertainty and the human quest for its antithesis. An important conclusion of his own quest is that a journey consisting of relentless and honest attempts to understand will always have uncertainty as its destination. This might be depressing if it were not for the fact that uncertainty is necessary for hope to exist.

We cannot hope for something we know for sure will never happen. And if something we hoped for happens, the hope for that thing vanishes. Indeed, our ability to go on hoping seems to imply that we either ignore, or are sceptical about, the certainties that we are given.

Ultimately, whatever our world view, it is hope that sustains us, and hope depends for its existence upon uncertainty. Yet we behave as though uncertainty must be killed, and gather an army of factual information as the chief weapon in this war that we constantly wage.

Changing the metaphor, we treat facts as though they were building blocks and we use them to create walls, towers, and suchlike to protect us in the "agoraphobia" that is our relationship with doubt

(Schulz, 2010, p. 169). Building blocks are, indeed, very useful if you want to build something rigid on solid ground. They are a less useful building material in areas prone to earthquakes and, if one is not building at all, but attempting to keeps one's head above turbulent water, being too attached to something as dense and gravity-bound can be fatal. One needs to be able to kick free. They are useful as an anchor, perhaps, but one needs an anchor rope that is long enough and not too heavy in its own right.

Allowed the status of certainty, facts become the arch-enemy of possibility. They kill potential and without potential there really is little point. Perhaps this is particularly true in the existential journey of the child. If I cannot bring anything of my own into this world, but only slot into some space predefined for me, then my life consists in being conceived of, and then constructed, by others. There has to be some self-invention. Just as the transitional object has to be created by the child, so does the child have to create himself. He may be given raw materials and there may be an expectation in the minds of others, but the child has to be able to adapt what is given and surprise expectations to some degree, or there is no meaning to his having been given an independent existence.

At the same time certainty, in the form of consistency and predictability, is crucial. The young person needs to feel a sense of being in control of something in her life. For that to be the case she must enjoy some degree of freedom, but she must also be able to predict likely futures. There have to be some predictable outcomes to her actions.

What is needed is a degree of predictability, particularly in the relationships between things. Up should be above down. The adolescent will appreciate boundaries, but not as things that cannot be crossed. Boundaries are things that, *if* you cross them, trigger an increasingly predictable qualitative change in state or behaviour.

As they grow, children and adolescents pass through different stages in their relationship with certainty. They are liable at times to latch onto facts with fierce and obsessive tenacity, and at other times will flatly deny the rationally and pragmatically obvious. This may seem to be a paradox, but it is not so. Or, if it is a paradox, it is one that we have to accept and live with. I am rehearsing two sides of an equipoise, or two sides of a coin. Much of what I do takes place at such a point of ambiguity, "halfway between everything" as Winnicott put it (1965, p. 29). It will probably prove to be a key paradox that I believe *passionately* that the ability to hold views *lightly,* or to hold opposing views simultaneously, is paramount. I am intolerant only of intolerance.

This Zen-like argument is meant to be experienced from within, rather than written about or read. It can be infuriating to listen to, but a clinician can only be of use to the young person in so far as she is able to live with this ambiguity. For this reason, if statistics are to be used, they must be understood. It may be helpful to know that, of a group of people in a given situation, ninety per cent have been shown to have a certain outcome, but it is of crucial importance to know that ten per cent had a different one. Whilst it would be unprofessional to ignore these statistics altogether, my patient must have an escape route from the certainty that they suggest, or there is nothing I can offer him.

If a person has a symptom—let us say a pain—and her doctor has looked at all the likely physical causes and drawn a blank, there is a danger that she will find herself trapped in her illness by a neurotic insistence (it may be hers or her doctor's) that the symptom must be caused by one thing *or* another. All I ask of my patient is that she entertain the possibility that emotions have a role in symptom amplification, at least. I am not requiring capitulation or surrender on this point. I do this by being absolutely confident that the mind and emotions are inseparable from the physical body and that, however confident we may become that a cause lies in one sphere, there will definitely be an element of causation in the other sphere also. This is certainty about uncertainty. I cannot prove it. Firm adherents of "evidence" would identify it as a belief.

The junior psychiatrist on an acute adult inpatient unit admitted a middle-aged man with depression. The man described his flight from an eastern European country following the publication of some of his anti-establishment writing and the young doctor felt himself to be in the presence of romance and danger as he wrote down the details. As time passed, information from a disgruntled lover contradicted much of what he had said. To this day the doctor does not know how much the man's flight was *from* the story and how much *into* it, though he has always been certain that his need for flight and his depression were intimately connected.

The importance of a clinician's ability to live and work with uncertainty needs to be emphasised. The poet John Keats, in a letter to his brothers written two hundred years ago, admired the ability of men "of Achievement … capable of being in uncertainties, Mysteries, doubts, without any irritable reaching after fact and reason" (Gittings, 1966, pp. 40–41). This description of the quality that Keats called "negative capability" was no doubt in Winnicott's mind when he referred to an essential "capacity in the therapist to contain the conflicts … and to wait for their resolution in the patient instead of anxiously looking around for a cure" (Winnicott, 1971b, p. 2). Irritable reaching after fact and anxious looking around for a cure are both phobic escapes from a suspended and uncertain state. The implication is that for anything to emerge one has to be able to live with the uncertainty as to whether it will do so or not.

Life is an uncertain business. Even the cells on the petri dish grow in a manner that is neither totally predictable nor totally random. Therapy, because it deals with living systems, is essentially an exploratory and creative process. Exploration requires a secure base, as attachment theory has taught us, but there is no security in terms of the anticipated outcome. The confidence shown by the clinician, then, must be a confidence in process coupled with an optimistic acknowledgement of the uncertain future. Perhaps the analogy is the jazz musician who has some landmarks and a great deal of artistry, confident that the result will be music but not entirely sure what he will do next.

It will be important for me to explain, perhaps in words, but more probably in demeanour and action, that I am not going to pretend to have understood everything about my patient—after all, I only met them an hour ago—but they have described some things which I recognise from elsewhere, and I have a hunch that I know roughly the direction we may be travelling. I may turn out to be wrong, of course, but that is fine. We can discover that along the way and adjust if we need to.

I don't mind my patient seeing me as someone who holds power and authority, but not over him. This is an authority and power, which may be of use to him while he regains his ground. I can prescribe medication if that is helpful, but I don't need to. I can write to the school and ask for a separate room for examinations, but I know that this, like medication, can sometimes create new problems for my patient, so we can decide together.

When seeking help, people often ask what turns out to be the wrong question, or present what transpires to be the wrong need, and then get fixated on the task of finding the answer to that question or that need. If the answer is withheld they are dissatisfied and frustrated. If they are given an answer, although they initially believe themselves to be satisfied, they develop a disquiet and discover that the problem still remains. They cannot understand why they are not satisfied or settled. It is a little like an addiction in which a substance that provides partial and short-term relief does not address the central issue. We are addicted to facts. Certainty is a charlatan and facts are the snake oil they peddle. The underlying need that they pretend to conquer is the need to relax into uncertainty. They provide an illusion of certainty, which is not the same thing. The comfort provided by this illusion is transitory and it is replaced by niggles of doubt that quickly swell to a clamouring for more facts.

So people (usually adults) often turn up asking for the wrong thing. In the consultation–liaison model (Lipowski, 1967, 1974) it is often necessary to respond to a question with a conversation that adjusts the question and takes things in an altogether more creative direction. This process works well if the person seeking assistance is prepared for the consultation–liaison approach but if they are not it often goes badly. The process is not helped in the slightest if the clinical service has a very limited number of answers. A parent says, "I want my child to behave better," and the clinician says, "This is ADHD; I suggest that you attend a parenting group and I can prescribe medication for your child." It is reminiscent of a conversation between two deaf people along the lines of, "Are you thirsty? No, it's Friday."

It generally seems to be the case that simple facts turn out to be wrong, or at least turn out to require significant qualification. A careful study of the gains from research often results in greater uncertainty about what can be said to be true. Perhaps I should regard facts as my friend after all. This cannot be the case until they are regarded by the ruling demographic as simple and crude resources, rather than the Grail.

It is also often the case that the more one researches the factual information around a choice the more complex the choice becomes. Factual information about available options can be less helpful in enabling resolution than learning more about the values, drives, and priorities of the people who will be affected by the choice.

Whilst there may be some occasions when a patient requires some factual information that can be readily and unequivocally provided, more often what they need is clarification and then soothing of more profound needs. This requires time and an openness to uncertainty, both as the medium in which we are living, and as the route most likely to lead us to resolution and autonomy.

Factual information can be of use to those functioning on the surface of things, but for the truly stuck or doubtful it can be more important to be able to demonstrate a comfort with paradox, uncertainty, and confusion. In this way we challenge the status quo which is, after all, something that the patient wants to move away from. We do not want homeostasis. We want a certain kind of instability so that a new and different position of homeostasis can be reached. Because change requires instability and therefore uncertainty, we must not only be able to tolerate uncertainty but actively seek it out.

Facts frequently do not answer human problems as effectively as companionship does. People have been told, perhaps especially recently, that they need facts. Professionals are even being told that facts are what they should be dispensing. We are all being told that problems can be solved by the provision of sufficient factual information. Admittedly, there are occasions when this is true, but my experience is that those occasions are rare, particularly when the problems are a complex mix of the inter—and the intra-personal, the psyche and the soma, thoughts, emotions, behavioural feedback loops, and suchlike.

If companionship and a renegotiation of the presenting dynamic are actually the more valuable, then some time will need to be bought in order to enable this.

Being with someone who is a) in a position of discomfort and, b) on a developmental trajectory requires a double message to be given:

1. This is how things are and they are bearable.
2. Things can change.

To say the first without the second would be sadistic. To say the second without the first would be to imply that the person must either be ready for uncontrolled change around them, or that they must change themselves, each of which can be experienced as an intolerable demand. The doctor demonstrates that life is bearable, and that things can improve. In this way she embodies simultaneously everything and nothing.

Laughter and irreverence

A medical student, during her four-week psychiatry placement, requested some experience with child and adolescent mental health services (CAMHS). She joined me with two patients only, and ventured an opinion: "I think I know the difference between child and adolescent psychiatry and general psychiatry." "Oh yes?" I said with genuine interest, thinking also that she had quickly generalised from an astonishingly small sample. "In child psychiatry there is more humour."

I was reminded of my own joy, as a medical student on acute paediatric attachment, when an infant caught the consultant with what seemed like an irreverent and well-aimed stream of urine. My similarly sweeping conclusion at the time was that children could bring consultants down to the ground in a way that no other patient could, and that this was excellent news for all concerned.

I like to joke with the families I see. Humour has a unique and pivotal position between the way things are and the way they might be. It signifies relief from the intolerable whilst the intolerable prevails, but it also destabilises. How many of us have experienced that very awkward moment when we catch ourselves laughing at something truly dreadful? It is the moment when we realise that the schism actually exists within us rather than our inhabiting a position securely on one or the other side of it. It is a shocking moment, but it carries with it immense hope as well as immense solemnity.

If I am on one side of a divide, then travelling from one side to the other might involve a scramble or a leap. If the division is within me then quite a different process is required. This is the therapeutic process. Therapy is the changing of something within, rather than either the manipulation of, or journey through, the exterior. The moment of laughter, then, frequently marks the shift inwards of attention. I cannot muster a vignette that would do justice to that moment. Jokes are discoveries and are best not rehearsed. (That is the artistry of the stand-up comedian: to rehearse the joke and then deliver it so freshly that it is experienced as a discovery—it is the same with a good whodunnit.) But some of the most satisfying moments are at that point where I have made some remark that has drawn a laugh, and then followed it by a reminder that we are here for a serious purpose. I will assert that these moments are therapeutic on the basis that that is how they feel, and I have almost invariably noticed rapport deepen at that point.

The dropping back from laughter to pain is like the dropping of electrons between energy levels; light is emitted. It is in these miraculous transitions that possibility is discovered. What is more, the flexibility that the clinician demonstrates—a facility in moving between states—is a model for the change that is required in the family.

The importance of laughter and irreverence, alongside ambiguity, in illuminating and permitting change, is mirrored by the significance of its absence when that is encountered. Anhedonia, being the inability to enjoy, can close off this avenue to a significant extent. This is what makes profound depression so difficult. It can be such a solid lockdown. In those circumstances one may need to find some other clue to the existence of hope, such as anger, for example, or the memory of a more optimistic state and a belief in reversibility.

If we can inhabit such solemn and such mischievous states at the same time, the solidity of the presenting problem is called into question as well as the nature of suffering.

The case for security

I have painted a picture of a laughing, confident clinician who is capable of tolerating uncertainty whilst taking upon himself responsibility for the emotional safety of a child travelling through dangerous and uncharted waters. It may be that the wise person appreciates insecurity (Watts, 1979) but most people need security at some level in order to be able to enjoy the insecurity introduced by exploration.

Bowlby (1988), Byng-Hall (1995), and others have written about the importance of a secure base in enabling the exploration of children in the context of family life and patients in the therapeutic situation. As a clinician, I also need to be able to explore and therefore need a secure base. I have found the importance of a secure base *for* the clinician to be less clearly enunciated than the requirement *of* them to provide it. Indeed, the literature that comes to mind jumps from the needs of the child and patient, over those of the individual clinician, and encounters the groundbreaking work of Menzies Lyth (1959), exposing the neurotic defences of organisations that require, evidently, their own sense of security. So the child requires security derived from his relationship with his parent, and in therapy they both require security derived from their therapist. The organisation develops its own defences against anxiety and these impinge on the employed clinician. One could interpret even the actions of societies, governments, and economies as reactions to their own insecurity, and there is no doubt that these can have negative effects on the culture of healthcare (Ballatt & Campling, 2011). Both employee and employer (and in the case of the healthcare industry, therefore, the patients and population) gain from the employment situation being a secure one (Herriot, 2001, pp. 13–16). Yet in my experience, as the economic belt has tightened expectations of reliability *from* the clinician have remained high whilst security of employment, remuneration, and esteem *for* the clinician have dwindled.

The tension created in the clinician who has to provide a secure base for her patient but has little security in her situation of work is obviously extremely regrettable. The task of *being with* can be effortful and at times will feel risky or dangerous at a profound level. It is very much easier if the territory of my relative safety is not merely contiguous with my physical body, as would be the case if we met in a neutral space, but extends into the room, redolent with visual and other cues. Whilst it may be possible to partition my inner self, keeping one sector secure while the rest roams, it would take superhuman solidity to be able to do this in the context of institutional, patient, and familial anxieties, without a plausible solidity in my physical, professional, and temporal surroundings.

I have chosen a career that repeatedly places me between tectonic plates and the resultant shearing forces are considerable. It has often felt as though it was my job to shift the focus of this shearing force away from the child. Sometimes that may be done by a well-chosen question, but often it requires me to inhabit and bear, at least to a degree, those forces myself. It is as though I insert myself into the shearing plane and then create an uncertainty there that I tolerate. This uncertainty acts as a lubricant, introducing the possibility—the hope—of movement. Imposing a spurious certainty at that stage turns the lubricant to glue.

Summary

- Facts are useful building blocks but they are not to be confused with certainty and, at times, they weigh us down.
- For the development of an individual existence there must be freedom of movement.
- There must also be a degree of predictability.
- Whatever we believe, it is hope that sustains us.
- We tend to search for certainty, but possibility and hope can only exist where there is uncertainty.
- If statistics and "facts" are to be used in relation to human growth, they must be understood such that the individual's room for manoeuvre can be demonstrated.
- This amounts to an attitude of irreverence towards the apparently immovable.
- Humour in the clinical setting reveals the creative space between how things are and how they might be.

- Treatment of people with mixtures of emotional and physical symptomatology is an area where the necessity of holding uncertainty is particularly obvious.
- Factual responses frequently do not answer human problems as effectively as do companionship and a readiness to explore.
- In order to be effective, the clinician requires a secure base.

CHAPTER FIVE

Thinking

T hinking does not happen only in people's heads. I use the word here to denote that process of reflective computation that happens in patients, clinicians, teams, and in the spaces between them. There are spaces outside of the individuals, yet inside the process. Here I shall explore thinking in this broader sense, distinguishing creative or therapeutic thinking, which can be done through action as well as cerebral activity, from more structured forms of thinking such as choosing. In particular I shall draw attention to thinking and playing as equivalent to one another.

The image comes to mind of iron filings on a sheet of paper. The people are the magnets under the paper, and the filings, thought-elements. A few may escape off to the side or fail to be pulled in, but almost all are drawn into a circle of influence that I may have already called the therapeutic episode. The magnets organise the thought elements into shapes, startling in their beauty—elegant, simple, and sufficient, like good scientific solutions or mathematical proofs. In the clinical context the point of the exercise is to benefit the patient-magnet, whose influence over the arrangement should gradually dominate.

In contemplating the ending of the treatment episode I shall stretch the analogy and suggest that we are dealing with electromagnets.

Gradually the power is turned down in the clinician and team so that they can leave an arrangement no longer reliant on their direct influence. At this stage in the process the analogy feels a little too static, fragile and grim, and we should probably let it go, but for the purpose of thinking about thinking, it is an image that may do the trick.

Thinking and playing

Creative and therapeutic progress is made when thinking can happen in a playing kind of way and, indeed, I consider creative thought and creative play to be the same thing. It is important to realise that someone can be thinking, in this sense, without conscious awareness of the fact.

On the other hand, I acknowledge that people can be helped to think in more conscious and structured ways and that this can also be helpful. CBT exploits the observation that what we think affects the way that we feel and encourages the choice of forms of words in our thinking that promote more positive feelings and behaviours. I use the image of a screw which, when twisted, advances in a given direction. If the angle of the thread is slightly changed the turning, which is just the same as before, now lifts our mood, thoughts, and behaviours rather than depressing them.

But that kind of thinking is not what I am talking about when I describe the role of thinking in *being with*. I shall employ a much broader definition of thinking which subsumes as a subset that species of linear-verbal thinking apprehended in our heads, talked about, and manipulated in CBT.

CBT now encompasses a wide group of therapies that share an ethos. It comes into this book in the same way that other therapies like pharmacotherapy and family systemic therapy do. It is one of the things that happens on the lines, rather than between them. I have said that *being with* is not a therapy, but an attitude conducive to the creation and maintenance of a therapeutic setting and the therapeutic practice of things called therapies.

If I am comparing thinking with playing, then I suppose I would see the approach to thinking used in CBT as rather like learning to play a game of chess or football. It is an excellent way of achieving a certain kind of result and, of course, if that is the result that is required then acquiring that skill is likely to be the most reliable way of achieving it. I do have concerns, though, about those children who have been taught to play a sport, a musical instrument, or a complex board game, to the exclusion of, a) *playing* which is the freer, more creative, and developmental activity, and, b) the less obviously creative but nevertheless important activity of boredom, or waiting to discover what it is that one is waiting for (Phillips, 1993).

Structured ways of thinking, then, can be the therapies and strategies that we teach our children, but it is important that we do not neglect to teach—or more likely to demonstrate and enable—them to *think* in a more playful and creative way. It is important that we do not give too much airtime to an activity that can look like thinking but is merely one way of thinking. The relationship between thinking and conscious cognition, in my view, is very similar to that between evidence and "evidence".

Choosing

Choosing can seem to be a sort of near-visible, deliberate form of thinking. Encouraging someone to think and requiring them to choose are, however, not the same.

We are told that choice is a good thing, and that we have a right, or possibly a duty, to exercise our choice, but when this happens we are not really encouraged to think for ourselves. We are effectively told how—and usually by a process of implication what—we should choose. Our aspirations are encouraged in certain directions and the range and nature of the alternatives offered to us are usually limited.

For example, we are provided with mortality statistics and are asked to choose in which hospital we want our operation to be performed. In this instance the following implications apply: statistics should inform our choice; the statistics provided are adequate for the purpose; choice should be based on a rational process; mortality is to be our main criterion of success or (more likely) failure; the hospital as a whole is the most powerful independent variable; responsibility for choice and, to some extent what flows on from it, lies with us.

Little wonder that we feel at the same time belittled and over-awed by the approach, because it derives from the well-worn manipulation of children by adults. The adult world is constantly dressing instructions up as choices: "Would you like to give me a hand with the washing up?" for example, cannot simply receive the reply, "No, thank you." A clever adult who has mastered this style of negotiation may say, however, "Oh, yes! I'd love to. I'll just pop to the shops for the milk first. Oh, and I'll drop in to see Mike on the way back."

Sometimes a pair of alternatives is offered that amounts to an instruction. "Would you like to read in bed, or have a chapter downstairs before you go up?" means, "You are going to bed in twenty minutes." This is an appropriate device in the management of children because it introduces them safely to the concept of autonomy before actually granting it. Towards adults, though, it is demeaning.

Less demeaning, but nevertheless largely unhelpful, is the approach that either flings a vast sprawl of information at the chooser or provides for comparison variables that simply cannot be weighed against one another. An example I have personal experience of is the choice of whether or not to undergo a risky antenatal screening process, given preliminary findings that suggested a medium risk of the foetus having Down's syndrome, and in a context of uncertainty as to how we would respond to a positive diagnosis at a relatively late stage of pregnancy. Another is the decision to immunise a child against a condition that she is unlikely to contract, effectively in order to maintain the "herd immunity" when the immunisation itself is thought to carry some risk. It could be regarded as irresponsible, unkind and dishonest to place on the slim shoulders of young parents the responsibility of choosing in these circumstances without supporting them with an ongoing relationship, and the encouragement and understanding they would need to be able to take into account, without feeling guilty and inadequate, their intuitions, values, and relationship to community.

It is my view that children are more aware of the power behind these choice tactics than most adults believe them to be. Children are as acutely aware of bullshit as they are of condescension and they are not fooled. The fact that they go along with an adult charade of compulsion dressed up as choice is likely to be because, a) it is more pleasant to feel as though you have some control (the accepted placebo) and b) they know that ultimately they will have to go along with it anyway. I say "aware" and "know" but I suggest that their awareness is at an instinctual level, not necessarily conscious, and that it produces a visceral response. They go along with it because they sense that the adults around them cannot conceive of a world in which they might not do so.

Sometimes I collude with, or even use, this approach, I must admit. The surly replies I receive come as no surprise and I consider them the young person's privilege, so I ignore any temptation to indulge in parental reprimand. This surliness may be primarily "because", as the child or adolescent sees it, they don't "like" the person talking to them.

But I am reassured when I examine this not-liking. What is there about me that is not to like? I might look or sound weird, that is for sure, but those are mere details and the patient knows this (the parents might be less aware; they may be very impressed with the efficiency of the waiting area and the fact that the professional has their name right first time, or they may be a little concerned because he has apparently cut his own hair). The child will be looking for some genuineness.

Let me put myself in the place of the child patient, for a moment. There would be a world of past experience and complexity that I still barely understand but I would have left behind any magical awe I had felt at adults' abilities to produce things or make things move. I would have reached the stage of disenchantment and would know that adults believe me ignorant of many things about which I have a deep and subtle understanding. These adults will have been busy telling me what is what for a long time, and denying their own fallibility, so I will have grown distrustful of their confidence and knowledge. I will have heard them tell me that everything is fine, and then go downstairs to shout and cry at each other. Or I might have heard them talking about me to someone on the phone. I would be scared because my own solutions, as well as those of my parents and teachers, had failed and I wouldn't be sure which was worse, them blaming me or blaming themselves and each other for that failure. "I have tried everything," I will have heard them saying, as though that were a) likely and b) a proof of my own alien nature.

I am taken to see a professional. I may arrive cynical—after all, this is another idea of my parents'—or I may manage to crank up my optimism one more time. I shall be interested in three things: 1) that the professional does not jump too quickly to a conclusion, 2) that the professional is interested, but not alarmed, by my situation, and 3) that the professional is capable of thinking or playing with ideas.

Being heard

David Goldberg and others (Goldberg, Gask & O'Dowd, 1989) developed a way of teaching GPs how to help a patient accept that there might be important psychological processes in play, despite the very physical nature of the symptoms experienced, and that these psychological processes might be the more useful focus of attention. The first step was making sure that the patient "feels understood". Genuine curiosity is necessary here. There may well be time pressures, but if a conclusion is reached, it must be reached sufficiently tentatively, and the more the conclusion is discovered by the patient, the better. It is a process of curiosity and facilitation. "Have you noticed this headache coming on at any particular times, at all?" "I wonder if the pain in your stomach might be a little bit the same."

Wondering

One of my psychodynamic training supervisors would periodically remind us of the value of "wondering". Rather than offering an interpretation as a suggested or likely fact, she would couch it in terms of, "I am not sure, but I am wondering if … ". What follows would then be incontestable, but more importantly would be effectively trying out a word or form of words for their potential as signifiers or elucidators of the patient's experience.

In the context of a play therapy I might start to wonder aloud, "If the tiny dragon might be feeling a bit scared, but a bit angry, too." During the assessment of a child who has missed a lot of school due to abdominal pain I might, at some point, say something along the lines of, "I have only heard a little bit of what has been going on, but I am beginning to get the impression that … may be …" The child can feel that there is room for movement, that I am listening and I am curious, that I have not taken their parent's description too much at face value, and that there is still time for them to discover, or express, or change, their own experience.

Talking

It may seem here as though I am using very grown up words. "I get the impression", for example, or even "I wonder". That may be the case. Françoise Dolto, attributed to language (especially for infants) an absolutely fundamental importance as the foundation and source of drives as well as the necessary basis of our ability to apprehend, understand, and integrate our experience (Dolto, 1987; Hall, Hivernel & Morgan, 2009, p. 68). Dolto was a firm believer in explaining things, even to babies. It may be that understanding and comfort are conveyed mainly in the tone of voice, and the words are for the speaker and the parent, or perhaps the provision of a word-handle enables the child to experience whatever-it-is as a thing that can be named and therefore managed.

I do not treat babies. I do, though, talk to children pretty much as I would talk to anyone. I am reassured by the response that I am understood at some level. Sometimes it is not the content that matters so much as the significance of being taken seriously. I may be operating on false faith but, provided I can retain my sensitivity in the moment, the sense of my own assurance is likely to reassure in its own turn. I would be watching the level of rapport, the deepening of which has been described as being "as near a one can ever get to scientific proof that … interpretation was correct" (Malan, 1979, p. 20). I know what it is like not to be understood. I would certainly not be looking for the ability to repeat or paraphrase. A child and her parents are likely to be able only to repeat a very small bit of what I have said and, in any case, this is not the learning-by-rote of poetry. The purpose is that she finds her own words for what happens in her life.

My test for the success of my approach would be to ask myself questions along the following lines: Did she feel understood? Does she think that I might be of some use to her? Does she want to come back?

If someone feels understood you can take him almost anywhere. In the context of stage or therapeutic hypnotism this may be done chiefly through mirroring, pacing, and then leading, but in a therapeutic setting in which hypnosis is not part of the contract (and therefore would be unethical) genuine understanding can perform a similar function.

It is crucial, in my view, not to rush towards a diagnosis or a cure, but to understand that this person is in something of a predicament. The diagnosis, if there is one, is merely an aide. The child must have it acknowledged, to them and in front of their parents, that they are a viable human being, and that they have hidden depths, both known to them and unknown.

Reticence and wondering, and this acknowledgement of hidden depths, both link to uncertainty, which is the topic of the previous chapter. It is a confident uncertainty that needs to be projected by the clinician at this stage, confident both of the fact that they are uncertain and in the company of this uncertainty.

Physical manipulation

Typically, when the family first enter, they will face me in various configurations which speak of family relationships, tensions, alliances. When the parents are ushered out, so that I can spend some time with the child, I typically move to a position more alongside. Not immediately, but as soon as it seems that we are looking together at something. This will require some negotiation. They may have already sussed me as a worthy ally, or they may still see me as an agent of "the man". Once I have been able to move, I am no longer looking at the child but with them at their experience. I am offering myself to them. They will find, hopefully, that I am curious to see things through their eyes, and confident that there is a way forwards in front of us. "This is what it looks like to me? Is that how it seems to you? These are the thoughts I am having about it. Are they useful, maybe? Well, let's see." I have already spoken of the position alongside as a metaphor for being with someone. Now I refer to a more concrete position alongside—at least temporarily—and it signifies to some extent the sharing of the discomfort as well as the lending of my thinking apparatus.

Not only am I opening out my thinking towards the predicament of the child, but by moving my position in relation to them and the now vacated chairs of their parents, I signify the fact that the world can be used as a sort of abacus for thinking, for ordering and reordering the elements of thinking and experiencing the changing relationships between them. This is what happens when a therapist asks someone to choose objects to represent members of their family, and then arrange them on the floor: reflecting and rearranging. We do the same every day as we let each other through doors, choose where to sit, make more or less eye contact.

Another way that children very obviously use their physical environment as a machine for thinking, is in play. The repetitive play of a child is often taken to be an attempt by them to master or understand something anticipated, remembered, or imagined. A child, given access to a doll's house and figures, and in the context of a discussion of their life, is likely to use these objects in an exploratory and reflective way, perhaps to see how ideas look in the outside world, or what happens when they are communicated in a tentative way with a receptive other. I am inclined to think that the same is true when the objects are manipulated in a less symbolic, or more "autistic" way, just that the use of symbolism is less adept. I cannot imagine a more economical or poignant communication of the wish for order in a confusing world, than the lining up of human figures in order of height, or of plastic cars in categories of colour.

Meaning

Another crucial notion, in the realm of thinking, is that of meaning. What do each of the parts of this story *mean*? Often, understanding the meaning given to ideas, events, observations, etc., explains the pressure behind their presentation. I shall return to meaning in chapters on diagnosis and treatment, but there could hardly be a better illustration of the importance of meaning than the instance of the transitional object— that scrap of material, for example, that is a smelly rag for someone not "in the know" but can cause a family to about-turn and drive back to the campsite when they were already halfway home. The meaning we attach to objects and actions enable them to be used as proxies in the task of achieving understanding and fluency in our lives, and this constitutes thinking. A clinician, sensitive to the power of these meanings, can join in the project and lend their own creativity, confidence, and experience. Failing to grasp meaning, though, can have unpredictable results. My father, using an illustrated phrase book in the Austrian Alps, failed to see the end of the arrow linking words and pictures. As a consequence he politely asked for a woman when what he wanted was a fork.

Summary

- Thinking happens within and between people.
- Creative thinking is really a sort of playing, and vice versa.
- The structuring of thought may be appropriate for certain specific therapies, but *between the lines* something more akin to creative play is necessary.
- The presentation of choices is the covert exercise of power over how and what we think.
- Children should be spoken to without condescension.
- If they feel understood they are more likely to experience hope and develop confidence in their ability to express, understand, and exercise some control over their experience.
- Thoughts can be embodied, manipulated, and understood in actions as well as words.
- Understanding this, and the very personal and unpredictable nature of meaning, enables the clinician to become a useful and powerful ally in helping the child to become unstuck.

CHAPTER SIX

Greeting and engagement

Although engagement may have its most obvious beginning as the clinician meets the patient for the first time, it may start earlier or later, and it certainly doesn't end there. Engagement, as a process, is ongoing. Like risk, engagement is dynamic and is revisited regularly as it deepens and thins, dependant on stages of treatment, errors of judgement on the part of the clinician, side effects of treatment, and suchlike. Like assessment, treatment, and even ending, engagement travels with us throughout the encounter and, to some extent, beyond.

Engagement is likely to become particularly important at sticking or turning points—rather as the grip between tyre and road becomes especially important during acceleration, turning, and braking.

Letters and outreach

Arguably, engagement will start with the idea of coming to CAMHS but this would be engagement with a fantasy. The first concrete contact is likely to be the appointment letter. Certainly, letters play a part in engagement. Everything about me and the service that is visible to or experienced by the patient and their system could be considered part of the engagement process.

It would be nice to be able to be out there and involved more directly in the process of pre-engagement and developing the public image of the service in which I work (and perhaps this book is partly an attempt to do this) but under current circumstances it is not going to happen. In any case, I suspect the gain would be small, and might even be negative, since the clinician dealing with large numbers of people, or in public speaking, or indeed writing a book, may not be playing to their strength, which should be in the task of being with small numbers, as I have described.

If letters go out correctly worded and provide sufficient notice, they will do enough towards initial engagement. I have known appointment letters to be sent two days before an appointment, or to the wrong address, and I am sure that often the parents' names are incorrect. Assumptions are made about "Mr. and Mrs. X", for example. We should do what we can to get this right. Leaving this task to computers is probably not good enough, and the pressure and burden of work on all clinic staff should be kept reasonable. Secretaries and frontline administration staff are part of the clinical team. I shall return to letters in chapters on treatment and ending as they are of more than passing importance.

The questionnaires that are often routinely sent out as a first response to referral in the public sector might be considered to have either positive or negative engagement effects. They belong more in the world of "paying the piper" (see Chapter Two) and utilitarian outcome measures (see Chapter Three). They can play a useful part in some kinds of assessment and sending them out before the first appointment may be considered an expeditious move, a way of using some of the waiting time, an opt-in filter, and the only way to get a genuine "time nought" baseline measure, but no one could claim that they were calculated to enhance engagement.

Decor

The potted palms in the entrance lobby to a private hospital come to mind. This can have too much of a corporate feel to me, too much like painting-by-numbers or the recorded message that tells me how important my call is to the (mechanical) receiver. It may be because I was shaped in a state-funded service, rather than the private sector, but I have developed a fondness for the dilapidated, and have come to consider the environment, part peeling institutional, part tatty-but-friendly home kitchen, as a context for the individuality of clinical work. If this were the frame of a painting it would be roughly limed timber or unpolished wood, rather than baroque gilt or stainless steel. I enjoy the response it draws from most patients and parents when I allude to this odd amalgam of the uniform NHS blue, attempts at the corporate, frank decay, and the heroic and unsung efforts of individuals. Most poignant is its redolence of continuation through failure. Perhaps the ability of a therapeutic process to survive therein becomes, in itself, some kind of model for the patient's use.

Manner and bearing

Though the decor can have an importance, provided the clinician is able to be bigger than it—superseding, eclipsing, ignoring it, or owning it with affection—their comportment will be the deciding factor once the first meeting has started.

> An experienced therapist was required to reapply for her own job owing to a cost-cutting reorganisation and she described some of the things she had wanted to get across in the interview. One was to explain how her specialised work began even as she stepped into the waiting room to call her patient, conscious that her handling of the greeting, her posture, and demeanour, such as how she held her shoulders as she led the way down the corridor, were important. Instead, she answered the call of the pay-banding criteria and talked about leadership. She felt she had betrayed an important loyalty.

What she had hoped to describe was an instance of highly skilled mentalisation. She knew that her patient, whom she would be already getting to know from body language and manner as well as from any information gleaned from the referral, would be affected by how he perceived the professional he had just met. Much would be projection, of course, but the clinician retains responsibility for how much she accepts, reflects, rejects, ignores, or amplifies projections, this work being as important to engagement as is the work of acknowledging but leaving behind pressures in one's own life.

All this rang true to me as she described it and was echoed with astonishing synchrony in a very moving letter that I stumbled across a few weeks later in the *British Medical Journal* (Hardy, 2013). In this brief response to an earlier article, a retired GP with a terminal illness wrote from personal experience as a patient: "We should not forget the importance of the greeting and the strategic significance of a walk down the corridor when dealing with our patients."

The setting

Where I work at present there are some tight corners and a flight of stairs to my room. I have developed a tendency to confirm a first name and provide a preliminary smiling greeting in the waiting room, sometimes shaking hands. I always make eye contact with the young patient, provided they allow it, and eye contact with at least one adult carer, but I typically say that I shall introduce myself properly upstairs and that I will just lead the way for the time being. This feels like something of a sub-optimal arrangement, but I think that my comfort with this slight shambles is itself a demonstration that one need not be perfect. We all do the best we can and will manage as things emerge and evolve. The contours of the encounter today will mimic those of the encounter overall, and how we handle today is likely to be how we handle our lives, broadly speaking.

The initial impression should be of a capable pair of hands. I hope to convey to my patient and their parents a sense of my own confidence that things can be OK, without in any way appearing glib. I want to show that I am at home in my profession, team, and work, without appearing blind to the arbitrariness or craziness embodied in that very environment and mentality.

If, as I prefer, I am seeing patients in the same room in which I write my notes, there will be an area of the room that is more office-like. The office chair will be set high, and there will be papers and other paraphernalia around the computer. I make a point of leaving this and sitting on one of the other chairs grouped in a rough circle. I do not go into these details to give the impression that I control them tightly, but more that I am aware of them. I think the effect of this move, apart from bringing me into a more acceptable geographical proximity, is to set out in a sculptural way my two predominant positions: one being the confident professional life, and the other being the unknowing, curious, and empathic companionship.

Not every clinician has the luxury of a room of his own. In truth I share it with a colleague, but I have absorbed her materials and she mine; there are territories that we adhere to between us. When I am in the room there is no doubt that I have extended myself to its boundaries. Once in it we are in my space. I am now freer to move and be vulnerable.

I have had to insist on keeping this room and, for reasons I have explained in Chapter Four, I am not embarrassed at having done so. The fact that I was successful points, however, to a seldom openly discussed privilege or power that attaches to my own professional training. I take advantage of this and argue that, in this way, I can be asked to work with some of the patients in the most troubling of situations, and provide a degree of supervision and support to others in the team.

Here we are, then, in my room.

A meeting of minds

I would like to be ready for the arrival of my patient and for them to sense that I have been prepared by the referral process, that the effort and time they have put into the process—itself often arduous, insane, and worrying—was not wasted or ignored. At the same time, and possibly more importantly, I want to be ready to hear the story from them directly and fresh. According the referrer's hypotheses the status of a) first clinical evidence and b) likely error, offers an early opportunity to demonstrate an open mind and familiarity with a confusion and conflict that may well mirror something in the patient's own mind.

As we sit down I would like the child and family to relax into the possibility of optimism without losing contact with the pain that has brought them and which they are about to explain or demonstrate. Humour can play an important part in achieving this necessary relaxation, but the instinct is a fine one and hovers on yet another balance. Irreverence and humour have to be tempered by sincerity that must be utterly genuine. It would not be my priority to make my patients laugh, though if they do so I have learned something useful, and maybe so have they.

I have heard actors and comedians, particularly when describing the difference between acting to film and acting to an audience, explaining the importance of the audience response. There is an element of performance to mental health work but there is nothing false about it. I am acting myself. Perhaps I am a method actor and have immersed myself in order to play the part as a natural expression of the me that I have evolved.

It is important to engage both the child and the parent. The former is almost always dependent upon the latter in getting out of school and into the clinic, so the parent must be convinced. On the other hand, the child or adolescent needs to be able at least to glimpse a uniqueness and independence in my initial appraisal of the situation. It would be rather discouraging were I to appear too much in thrall to the parents or teachers, or if my response were too demonstrably what those people appeared to want or, indeed, too obviously its antithesis.

Typically a child will have heard by this stage, and over the years, innumerable things said about him, but will have said extraordinarily little about himself, other than very privately. Junior schools can some-times be the only place where a child has publicly painted a picture or told a story about himself. The very private statements, initially out-and-out fantasy (the ability to fly, the running battles across the hill, the large family of dolls to feed, teach, or punish) are crucial, but they have rarely been made sincerely public. Sometimes, if they are, the adults react with scorn or fear. I have encountered families where the parents were very worried that their child's imaginary friend was a symptom of early psychosis. The situation is not helped if the teacher is also afraid that this might be the case.

What adults typically fail to understand about play is that it is at the same time both throwaway and serious. The child often has to keep the seriousness of their play hidden from the adults. Their sense that the adults will not be able to handle it correctly is all too frequently justified. As well as taking play too seriously, ignoring, or scorning it, families make decisions about family members, young and old. It is as though they take even their own play too seriously. Often a consensus forms that this parent was the martyr, that one the saint; this child the clever one, that one the stupid one, etc. These agreements may crystal-lise out of no more than a discomfort with suspense. If every family has to have an idiot, they seem to have said, let us get it over and done with and know who it is as soon as possible. People need to know the role they are playing. The problem is that in play one needs to be able to let it drop, and these roles can become fixed. A role that works for the fam-ily may not be in an individual's best interests, particularly as they start to attempt the shift of emphasis from their local microcosm towards fitting into the wider world. It is important for the family's survival stratagem to be credited whilst allowing the child an escape route from it—face-saving for the family, perhaps, but plausible, attractive, not too daunting, for the developing individual.

The young person needs to feel heard, and to acquire a sense that I am getting somewhere but that I have not jumped prematurely to any conclusions, that I am operating comfortably within my own zone, that I am confident. This is not a confident possession of knowledge but confidence within my own skin, remaining unshaken by the material.

She also needs to be able to see that I am comfortable in handling her parents, perhaps that I have caught a glimpse of the problem that she has encountered in managing her parents' behaviour or feelings. This must be done without any suggestion that I am disparaging the parents. On the few occasions that I have made the mistake of commiserating with the young person in her task of managing a parent, I have felt a distance open up. If engagement has started well, then we can each sense this loss of rapport with some minor alarm and sadness.

At the same time as achieving this delicate balance of convincing the child of my worthiness without overstepping the mark, I have to do the same with the parents, and they will measure my worth in a different way.

In my experience the parents fall into two broad categories: those who are bringing the child through their own agency and motivation, and those that have been sent. The former have often had to push for this appointment and as far as they are concerned it is long overdue. To borrow from Berne (1964), these parents are squarely in the position of parent. If they have brought the child because they have been told to—often by their child's school—they are themselves, to some extent, in the role of child.

There is less of an engagement tightrope walk when parents are in child mode. Just as the child is interested in my ability to "handle" their parents, these parents will be pleased to see that I can handle the school. Sometimes they are openly relieved that the process of assessment may take some considerable time, because they know that this will take pressure off them and their child. Or they will be relieved to see that I am in no way intimidated by special educational needs coordinators. In this situation initial engagement is usually relatively easy, the challenge coming later, in the treatment or the discharge phase, because for those to take place it becomes necessary to notice the absent or projected parent role and support its proper readoption by the parent. Parents will also be less easy to farewell if they are still covertly using me as a benign and powerful parent for themselves.

Of course, this last amounts to the parents having attempted, albeit unconsciously, to obtain therapy for themselves through the attendance of their child. I suspect that a frequent cause of failed engagement or treatment in child and adolescent mental health is to do with unmet need of this kind in the parent. If this is simply a need for factual information, skill acquisition, or a change in perspective it may be managed, but if it is a more profound need it is destined to frustration as what they get will amount neither to their phantasy nor to the therapy that they no doubt require for themselves.

Parents in parent mode, in contrast, are unlikely to be impressed by my scepticism and mischievous disrespect for the rather arbitrary power structures in which we live. Generally, they are looking for reassurance that I am familiar with these power structures and will faithfully follow the latest guidelines. They want to know that I share their sense of urgency in sorting this problem out, and they want to see signs of certainty and conclusion much earlier than the child does. My sense is that they are much more convinced by the accoutrements and stage props of medicine than the child is. Where the child will instinctively be looking for subtlety, the parents will be more impressed with the "flashing" of some knowledge. I am not good with figures, but percentages can be useful at this point. They know then that they are in good hands.

I am put in mind of Antoine de Saint-Exupéry's *The Little Prince* (1945), in the opening pages of which the author describes the difference between the subtle and emotionally intelligent requirements of the child and the relatively banal interests of the adult.

The process of engagement, therefore, is a balancing act in which the pressurised (adult) agenda has to be met, acknowledged, and convinced that it will be taken seriously by someone capable, whilst those in the child position need to be reassured that everything can be slowed down by someone sufficiently powerful and sufficiently at home in their own field to be able to live with the suspension of certainty.

It must be visible to all that I can accommodate the parent's views as well as the child's, even if they are apparently inconsistent. Interestingly this can fairly easily be achieved by seeing them separately. Child and parent may each know, respectively, that the other has a view inconsistent with their own, yet they seem almost invariably to accept that I have spoken with them each and taken them each seriously. They do not seem to need any explanation of what my conclusion is, or how I have been able to reconcile these views within my own mind. There are exceptions—parents who want to know that the child has been honest, for example, by which they mean that his story accords in factual detail with their own.

There is something of the confessional in this, it seems to me as I describe it now: each going into the booth with a belief that they will be listened to and somehow helped, some transgressive curiosity as to what the other has said, perhaps, but respect for the rules of confidentiality and ultimately happy that their curiosity be kept unsatisfied.

A capacity for internal as well as external equivocation is necessary, though is frequently much less welcomed by the parent than the child. The parent, no doubt, is further removed from the transitional phenomena, which are, after all, the child's, and has been more thoroughly acculturated to the fact-based world. This tendency to equivocate—to ambiguate—is evident in much of what I have to say.

One value of having two parents who manage to either stay together, or at least remain in constructive collaboration, is that it models the coexistence and possible reconciliation of opposites. Often, slight differences between parents emerge and are magnified, over the years or in the child's mind, and can become polarities. The fact that these polar opposites continue to communicate, cohabit, and even (horror of horrors) copulate, confronts the growing child with the possibility of reaching a relatively settled situation where there is, Yin-Yang-like, some black in the white and white in the black and the two entwined. A confusing situation inside the child is seen to be reconcilable in the outside world in a way that might in time be internalised.

In conjoint couples therapy, where each of the two therapists may start predominantly aligned with one of the pair, their ongoing collaboration can begin as an object of curiosity and incomprehension for the patient couple, and graduate towards a usable model for their future relationship.

In engagement, the clinician's ability to accept two or more differing views without collapsing or exploding can offer hope to the child and her parents. "This guy might be able to survive us and, by the way, how does he do it?"

Finding myself talking in terms of couples therapy draws my attention to the choice of the word "engagement". Therapy is not a marriage, if for no reason better than that a) it would be polygamous, and, b) the parties must part before death and, hopefully, without the trauma of divorce, but the analogy is an interesting one. Where engagement to be married and engagement into treatment may be similar is in the fact that, 1) they are both preparatory to a contract, the primary purpose of which is creativity, and, 2) the prognosis of the relationship is hugely improved if there is some element of enjoyment of one another from time to time but, at least in love-marriage, particularly during the negotiations that amount to engagement.

Proxy

I think that it is possible, to some extent, to engage on behalf of someone else in the team, though the requirements are significant. This is necessary if the team has divided the roles of assessment and treatment. The principal requirement is that there be a high level of team cohesion. If the initial appointment is followed either by a ridiculously long (sadistic/negligent) wait then any engagement will be more than lost and may well have soured to its opposite, undermining anything else that might be offered later. This is similarly true if promises made at the outset turn out to be empty. The biggest mistake here is to fall into forgetting that treatment is a personal thing that takes place in a personal relationship. The engaging clinician must have an evident and actual close working relationship with anyone else who is to work with the patient or family. In this way, not only explicit promises about what will happen next will be fulfilled, but also the "promise" of a certain quality to the relationship. I return to this in Chapter Eight.

The basis for a therapeutic relationship

When the patient and his family leaves the consulting room, provided they have not been turned away or referred on to someone else, they have acquired a powerful therapeutic companion. In relation to the clinician they have just met, the young patient may sense the following:

1. She is experienced in the field of the emotionally painful and the poorly understood.
2. She listens, has heard, and, perhaps, begun to understand my situation.

3. She is clever enough to avoid taking sides or jumping to conclusions.
4. She is comfortable with me in my own discomfort—to the extent that she has not rushed into trying to eradicate it.
5. She has some of my discomfort in her now.
6. She would like to see me again.
7. Therefore she believes that this discomfort is survivable, and
8. She doesn't find me totally unpleasant or frightening, and
9. She may be able to help.

This invites the following conclusions:

1. My discomfort may be survived by me and others, and
2. It may not be permanent.
3. I may find out something new about myself and how I fit in.
4. My parents/friends/teachers may find out something new, and
5. They may yet find me acceptable.
6. These things haven't happened yet, but are possible.
7. Things may not be as bad as everyone thought.
8. I would like to return to see this person again.

This is a good start. The price is commitment on the part of the clinician because the trust that this engagement reveals and has been placed in them must not be betrayed. The reward is immensely satisfying work.

Summary

- Engagement neither begins nor ends at the first physical encounter but is an ongoing and dynamic process.
- The first actual encounter with the service is important.
- The first personal encounter with the clinician is even more important.
- Manner and bearing are part of the clinician's art.
- The clinician requires for this work a secure work environment to meet and hold their internal secure base.
- There is an element of performance to the work that detracts not at all from the sincerity of the clinician and the encounter.
- Engaging the child and the adult are parallel activities.

- Being recognised, valued, heard, and to some extent understood, in an encounter that the clinician enjoys, are important aspects of therapeutic engagement.
- Engagement by proxy can take place provided there are close working relationships between clinicians and promises are kept.
- Engagement is the foundation and backbone of a therapeutic relationship.

CHAPTER SEVEN

Assessment and diagnosis

Assessment and diagnosis are not the same. I shall explore the nature of assessment within the clinical context, considering several aspects of assessment, including its relationship with diagnosis. I shall then think about some implications of assessment for the therapeutic relationship and the relationship between the patient and the patient's own self, and conclude that clinical assessment is best if it is absorbed into an intelligent relationship in which there is an ongoing duty of care. In this situation, assessment is less likely to cause harm to the developmental process and more likely to inform the overall management in a dynamic way. Clinical risk assessment will be thought about as a useful illustration of some of these ideas.

Assessment

Assessment is used far beyond the clinical setting. One can assess the damage after a storm, for example, or carry out self-assessment for taxation. In the clinical context one should be assessing the need for clinical intervention. Other services, most notably education services, request information derived from clinical assessment in order to inform their own practice. Leaving aside which budget should fund assessments

98 BEING WITH AND SAYING GOODBYE

serving non-clinical purposes, there is the fact that, in order to carry out a clinical assessment of a child, I have to engage with them in a clinical context. I then owe them a duty of care and they have become my patient. Consultation–Liaison work is somewhat different in that the relationship is with the professional requesting the consultation, although I owe the child an indirect duty of care in relation to any advice I give. The assessment is not of the child or of the professional, but of the question asked.

Assessment is more, even, than determining the need for a clinical service. It should also take in the readiness of the patient to engage, the means by which care or treatment can be provided, and its likely risks. There is little merit, and some potential for harm, in assessing someone and proclaiming that they need a specific treatment, if that treatment is not realistically available to them.

Diagnosis and diagnostic formulation

Diagnosis is a word whose meaning, in the context of healthcare, we have allowed to thin to the point where it is generally taken to refer to the provision of a label. It is regarded as a mainly medical activity, and the label is sometimes called a "medical diagnosis" or a "psychiatric diagnosis". I think that most doctors experience some disquiet at this simplification, but it is difficult to resist the pressure of expectations.

If an assessment comes up with a noun for the patient's predicament— such as depression, hypertension, autistic spectrum disorder—then I think the consensus would now be that it has generated a diagnosis. The action of diagnosing produces a diagnosis, whereas the action of assessment can produce a diagnosis, but need not necessarily do so, and should always do more.

Psychiatrists also talk about "diagnostic formulation" and this blurs the distinction I have just made. A diagnostic formulation, properly done, is a genuinely gripping description of the patient's predicament, taking into account crude and subtle impacts as well as inherent strengths and weaknesses, locating the patient's problem in time and in dynamic interaction with its context, and showing an interest in uncertainty and the future. In fact, diagnostic formulation is a genuine attempt at "knowing" or "perceiving" "through" or "thoroughly" (diá—gignóskein: Onions, 1966) and comes close to a *being with* approach to assessment.

It is a shame that diagnosis, on its own, should have become such a mean little word. Indeed, doctors who would argue with what I have said about it might find that I agreed with them to a large extent. Many of the limitations of medicine are not intrinsic, but have been visited on it because of the preconceptions and taboos held by non-medics. The term "medical model", when used pejoratively, is almost certainly being oversimplified. Equally, the actual model can be, and, I think I am suggesting here, often is misapplied. I may or may not have been trained into reductionism, but I am quite sure that I have, at times, had reductionism thrust upon me. I am asked, "Does she have X?" and what I would like to say is something along the lines of, "I have got to know her a bit and can see that she is struggling with a number of things. I think that we can help her with some of them and I shall let you know if there is any assistance that you could provide." Doctors, collectively and individually, haven't always helped because we are not immune to hype, fashion, and suchlike, and particularly when under pressure, have to ration our philosophical and relativistic thinking.

The attaching of labels derives partly from our collective reluctance to admit uncertainty. "Is it or isn't it, doctor?" I imagine myself in court, or on the morning current affairs programme, and how shoddy I would look if I showed even the slightest uncertainty in answering such a question. But we are talking about biological systems and sub-jective experience, each of which is notoriously complex and uncertain. I should at least be able to answer the question with, "It depends what you mean," without losing my professional standing.

Views differ within the psychiatric profession as to exactly what a diagnostic formulation is or should contain. Since most agree that it should include a consideration of the pros and cons of possibly appli-cable diagnoses, one could conclude that speculation, uncertainty, and debate are at the core of psychiatry, and are actively encouraged. The item most frequently left off, probably, would be prognosis. This might almost be excusable if one retained the image of the frock-coated physi-cian gravely stroking his chin and proclaiming on the duration of useful life remaining. If, on the other hand, one thinks of prognosis as the pro-vision of information on likely risks or outcomes of treatments versus non-treatments, this component of the formulation is revealed to be the bedrock of informed consent.

It is easy to see what an impressive range of information a good diagnostic formulation can cover, and how neatly it can summarise.

Achieving this within an hour or two of talking with the patient is in my view such an undeniably skilful achievement that it is likely to be done badly more often than well. To expect oneself to be capable of it might almost amount to hubris. At the very least it demands skill and time.

Precision

I suspect that, overwhelmingly, everyone is trying very hard to make the world a better place. I do know that while I am busy in clinical practice a large number of doctors, scientists, sociologists, ethicists, etc., are striving to make clinical practice more safe, effective, ethical, and affordable. It may be that, collectively, we are working too hard. There is a risk of developing a positive feedback loop driving us in one direction. More efficient and more powerful treatments increase the ethical importance of equal access, but may also be more dangerous. Failures in either just, or safe, delivery increase public alarm and fuel the demand for precision in diagnosis, further economies (not taxation, generally), better targeted treatments, more surveillance, etc.

In other chapters I hope I have explained my reservations in relation to certainty and too narrow a definition of evidence. It should come as no surprise—and I hope you will not be too incredulous or scandalised—when I say that I do not consider precision in diagnosis, or even assessment, to be the main goal. I want us to remember that helping a child forwards is the main goal. If we are going to use a drug with serious side effects we must absolutely take notice of the scientific information about the effects of that drug, good and bad. But in deciding whether or not to attach the diagnosis or use the drug we must look further than measures, cut-offs, and the like.

Diagnostic criteria, in order to be useful in research, can become too narrow to be very useful clinically. Biological and subjective systems can justifiably defy pigeon-holing. Behaviour and outcome in an individual cannot be reliably and accurately predicted by large trials, however well conducted. Why have hugely respected clinical academics walked off international panels devising diagnostic schedules? Could it be that we are trying to be too precise?

If you ask me if so-and-so is "depressed", my answer will depend on what you mean. Do you mean right now? What sort of depression are you talking about—mild, moderate, or severe, and in which diagnostic schedule? Even if you drill down into the diagnostic manual, you are still likely to find that a number of the required features involve value-judgements and words like "marked", "usually", "commonly", or "great".

Assessment and power

Despots will not allow themselves to be put in a situation where they are being assessed unless they are totally confident that they can control the outcome. The very fact of one person being in a position to make a judgement in relation to another is an assertion of power. The assessee may be a supplicant, wanting or needing something, or, alternatively, they may not want the assessment at all and fear its consequences. Personal—and sometimes highly personal—information is all going one-way, and attempts at innocuous self-disclosure on the part of the assessor will do little to assuage this. The process of assessment calls to mind the uncomfortable experience of being-seen-without-seeing and the shocking fate of Rumpelstiltskin once his proper name was discovered.

Knowing the name of something often brings power over it and one might be forgiven for thinking, therefore, that naming the illness is all the more laudable. But these names are just our best guesses and, worse than that, there appears to be constant confusion over whether diagnostic labels apply to the condition or to the person. We all know that it should be the former. The intention in labelling an illness is for us to obtain power over *it* on behalf of the patient but, despite constant effort and reminders, we keep slipping up and call people with schizophrenia "schizophrenics" and those with depression "depressives". Labelling the person rather than their problem bequeaths stigma and ransacks self-esteem.

We may not want others to name us or our characteristics. Apart from anything else, it may not be in our interests for this information to be broadcast to others, including (perhaps especially) our parents who are already in a substantial position of power over us. We may even want to remain ignorant of some details about ourselves, at least for long enough to acquire sufficient core self-esteem, and the knowledge and skills necessary to manage the information and what flows on from it.

The clinicians and the parents want power, of course, because they are scared. Quite possibly more scared than the child. But they should not take power in such a way that it strips away what trace of healthy power the child had previously. We also need to be very cautious of using the diagnosis of illness to empower the child, or to enable them to circumvent power, as this risks the very dangerous dynamic of illness-behaviour whereby the only power accessible is the power that comes from the rather pyrrhic victory of being ill. This can be one of the adverse outcomes of assessment and reasons for resisting diagnosis, expanded on below.

> The mother of a very hyperactive child with whom the primary school struggled admirably, habitually started the consultation in the corridor to my room, talking cheerfully and loudly about family difficulties; she forgot appointments, rummaged through heaps of paper in her large handbag, and leapt from topic to topic such that it was hard to decipher what she was saying. She did not suffer from mania. A new clinic was established for the assessment of attention deficit hyperactivity disorder (ADHD) in adults and, after a while, I wondered aloud to her whether she would like a referral for herself. I reasoned that, if the label could be applied to her and if treatment were to help, it might enable her to provide a more consistent environment for her child, instead (I thought, more privately) of the rather chaotic and unpredictable one prevailing. She thought about it and at the next appointment declined, explaining that, if the condition were diagnosed in her, she would feel such overwhelming guilt that she would be unable to parent at all.

How hard should I have persuaded her? Was there a safeguarding concern? I had to accept that she was very possibly right. The harm in diagnosing her might well have outweighed the benefit. After all, a chaotic, lovable, and loving mother is probably better than a totally absent or perpetually distraught one—or no mother at all. And yet she was prepared for that process of diagnosis and subsequent treatment to be applied to her child. Parents often give to their child what they have been denied themselves. She at least was able to accept and love a child with a diagnosis in a way that she would not have felt accepted or loved in the same situation.

The Māori word *whakamā*, referred to in Chapter One, literally means "to make or move towards paleness", and relates to loss of *mana*, this being the power that keeps us standing tall. As Metge (1986) illustrated, when attempting to help someone it is important to do so in such a way that you do not cause or contribute to their *whakamā*. We should meet our patients as equals and, if they accept us, stand alongside them in the face of their difficulties.

Considerable power is wielded in the process of assessing a child, such that a) it is likely to be an uncomfortable experience, b) not freely consented to, and as a consequence of which the child is likely to experience, c) a breach of their confidence, and, d) a possible loss of social power and self-esteem. All of these risks are taken on in the belief that assessment will lead to an intervention that will prove to be in the child's greater interests. We had better hope that this turns out to be the case!

The meaning of assessment

In exercising my duty of care I need to take notice of, and some responsibility for, the meaning that the patient takes from the process. Even if a label can obtain resources for him and serves his interests in that sense, with a few exceptions I still prefer not to attach the label to him until I am confident that he has understood and agreed to it.

We should explore what the meaning of a diagnosis would be for each party. A diagnosis may represent fallibility or it may imply treatment, for example. It may mean money and resources. It may attribute or absolve from blame. "Giving the child a diagnosis" might confirm in everyone's mind that the child is or contains the problem. Even that can cut both ways. It may not all be bad. It may organise the family system towards adapting to the child, instead of to a grandparent or to the parents' careers, for example. It may enable the child to revise their priorities around academic achievement. But it often results in an insistence on the correct treatment being "applied" to the child in order for the prevalent expectations to be maintained, or in a magical bid for a new life for the family, and this may not be in the child's best interests.

To parents, a diagnosis of ADHD in their son might mean the following:

- "What happened to his dad will happen to him" (*death aged twenty-three from drug overdose*).
- "It's not my fault" (*not my genes/I am a good parent*).
- "It IS my fault."
- "It is his dad's/his mother's fault."
- "He will have to take medication" (*and taking medication means …*).
- "He will need support at school" (*off to battle*).
- "Other children will call him 'psycho'."

- "His life will be difficult" (*We are going to be worried about him forever*).
- "That is why he argues when I tell him to do things" (*He is wrong*).
- "He is doing it for attention" (*He is wrong*).
- "Poor lamb, and I thought he was just being naughty" (*I was wrong*).
- "I haven't been paying him enough attention" (*It is my fault*).
- "There is something wrong with his brain."
- "Other parents will want their children to keep away from him."
- "We can get Disability Living Allowance or a bigger house."
- "Here we go! We didn't give things these fancy names in my time."

For the child it might mean:

- "I am ill."
- "I am naughty."
- "I am cool."
- "Who am I?"
- "I will have to go with the other psycho kids who take medication at lunchtime."

And so on.

These are just suggestions. Two vignettes with a bearing on the meaning of illness and symptoms are recounted in the next chapter. In particular, Stephen's story tells of how a diagnosis can become one of the most powerful *dramatis personae* in our lives. When we assume it to be the enemy, we find ourselves grieving its absence.

If it becomes a friend, though, it can be a very dangerous one. I still remember, from medical school, the abdomen of a man with Munchausen's syndrome, criss-crossed with scars, and the mixture of satisfaction and confusion with which the surgeon pointed out that internal scarring from earlier unnecessary operations could cause constrictions genuinely requiring urgent surgical intervention.

The important thing is to get alongside the patient and find out what each of these things—illness, assessment, treatment, and so on—means for them. This is part of the assessment and needs to be kept in mind when decisions are made about management.

As a society we are deeply confused in relation to factitious and induced illness, no doubt partly because of simplistic segregation of cause and effect and consequent inference of blame. Somatisation has been defined as a "tendency" with the assumption that it resides in the patient (Lipowski, 1986). It is not as simple as this. I prefer to see it as a process predisposed to by tendencies which include those of the clinical services to assess and diagnose, and of certain patients to attribute and present their subjective experience in certain ways.

With time and help a patient and her family may discover that they don't want or need a diagnosis. Under different, though frequently entwined circumstances, they may need help in accepting a diagnosis and responding to it.

Adverse effects of assessment and diagnosis

That we should want to know the diagnosis or cause of a difficulty is assumed to such an extent that clinicians, parents, and patients can all launch themselves into assessment automatically, without having sufficiently considered the costs and benefits for all concerned.

Encouraging and enabling negative illness-behaviour is not the only adverse effect of assessment and diagnosis. A diagnosis can be something of a depth charge in someone's life with the potential to dramatically shift the balance of power in a family, for example. Self-esteem may be deeply affected. Future career choices can be restricted. Some of these effects may be inevitable or for good reason, but it should at least alert us to caution in relation to over-enthusiastic assessment as well as, if we do assess, spurious precision and categorising.

Much of this argument applies more in mental health, and in children, than it does in other areas of clinical practice. If it were simply that the child and illness were two entities that had got stuck to each other, and if the illness could, as a consequence of being diagnosed, be painlessly removed without damage to the child, then we could be less ambivalent about assessment. In mental health, though, the problem encountered is intertwined with selfhood, so removal of it may not be possible without collateral damage. Often, indeed, we are effectively scrutinising and passing judgement on intrinsic characteristics and not illnesses at all.

Everyone feels on their back foot coming to the child and adolescent psychiatrist. The parents are worried that they will be told that they have caused the problem and that they are "bad parents". The child similarly is likely to be feeling that they are either broken or faulty, or are defiantly fighting off the idea. The whole family, which has a collective self-esteem all of its own, is concerned at the possible verdict that will be passed on it and, in efforts to preserve its own dignity may collude with, or invite collusion with, a process that locates the difficulty squarely within the child.

There is an assumption, generally, that confidentiality about the existence of a diagnosis does not apply to the privacy barrier between children and their parents. We believe that we are well prepared for the conversation about what we disclose to parents when it comes to risk, but we seem to have assumed that it is fine to tell parents that their child has a diagnosis of depression, anxiety disorder, Asperger's syndrome, etc. This assumption may not be a safe one. Not all families are safe places and not all of us have the strength to turn our fear into compassion.

It should follow from what I have said above, that the potential harms of assessment need to be taken seriously before one even comes to the potential dangers of treatment.

There may be some particularly unhelpful practices. One would be the assessment that provides labels but no meaningful treatment or support. In these situations the dangers I have described would not even have a potential treatment benefit to weigh against them. These are likely to create disenchantment, at the very least, and decrease the likelihood of further help-seeking when the need is perhaps even greater.

Sameenah came from a family in which more than mere traces of anxiety, eccentricity, and intellect, were visible over two or three generations. She was referred with severe panic attacks mainly in exam situations, but resulting in wider isolation from her peers at school. She did not want psychological treatment for her anxiety because several years ago she had been seen at the anxiety clinic and she and her mother had not found it helpful, largely due to the experience of being scrutinised through a battery of questionnaires. An eclectic process, over a period of time, and including wide-ranging assessment and exploration of options including medication (which did not help much), allowed trust to develop. This trust was used to persuade her, against her instincts, to have another go at the anxiety clinic. After a few months' wait she was seen by a student who administered several questionnaires and then, through an impersonal process, she was assigned the opportunity of group treatment which she rejected. She returned to the psychiatrist moderately disgusted and the work of rebuilding trust was resumed, along with revision of basic approaches to panic, and conversations that effectively validated her as a human being. She obtained some qualifications, left school for college (which she could tolerate) and took up part-time work (at which she excelled).

The initial assessment in this case did not elucidate the breadth or subtleties of the patient's predicament, did not lead to either therapeutic engagement or useful treatment, and served to put her off mental health services.

An experienced psychiatrist was on holiday with friends and was introduced to a family in which one of the children had a tic. Someone asked the child why she was pulling a funny face and the psychiatrist, believing he was doing her a favour, said, "Oh I think it is just a tic." He later learned, to his chagrin, that this caused the girl's parents more than transient consternation.

It may at times be better not to be too clever. Outside of the context of an ongoing clinical relationship, and the likely provision of information and treatment, a diagnosis may not be helpful. There is an aspect of assessment, particularly if it is conducted in a summative rather than a formative way, which can be for the subject rather like being laid bare.

One of the dangers of diagnosis is that it encourages the idea that the treatment is for the disorder, rather than for the patient. The emphasis on coding and "payment by results" has moved us towards diagnosis-specific treatment pathways. This reductionist approach is, to my mind, disrespectful of the patient. It implies that the person does not, in themselves, warrant assistance whereas the disorder does. It denies the fact that the patient's journey—the person's journey—is a long one, only one chapter of which touches the CAMH service. It makes it more difficult for integrated, flexible, and sensitive treatment to be provided. It colludes with the process of labelling the patient rather than understanding their predicament.

I should not be too dramatic. I hope that the majority of people referred to CAMHS benefit, on balance, from what follows, but I am confident that there are people who have not benefited, some who have carried doubts about themselves because of the fact of being referred, or others whose difficulties have been perpetuated or exacerbated in some way through misunderstanding of, or insensitivity towards, the process, or a lack of determination or support in conducting it.

Whilst I am, a) noting the possible harms of assessment, b) cautioning, as I shall in a moment, against assessment without treatment, and c) suggesting that treatment may often be more effective with less precision, it is terribly important to be clear that treatment without assessment would be reckless. Assessment is an absolutely essential prelude to intervention.

Given, then, that we have to assess, we must do what we can to minimise the harm and unpleasantness that can stem from it.

Resisting diagnosis

If, after considering all of the above, we decide we can safely carry out some sort of assessment, is our aim going to be to make a diagnosis? I hope not. Diagnosis is the servant, not the master, and our aim should always either fall short of diagnosis or go further than it.

The pitfalls, negative meanings, and adverse effects are enough reason to be cautious about diagnosing. Given that there are internalised and external pressures upon health professionals (and not only doctors) to diagnose, readiness and ability to resist these pressures are important. This can be hard work and time consuming. If assessment has been done well, along the lines of diagnostic formulation and with an attitude of *being with*, it can often inform the management plan without actual diagnosis. When I have asked patients and their parents what they would choose if they had the option of either treatment without diagnosis or diagnosis without treatment, they have invariably chosen the former. If one is engaged properly in the relationship, whether it is called an assessment or not, one can find that the problem has been solved or abandoned without diagnosis or even a specific or identified treatment.

Doctors sometimes get the blame for "medicalising". I am not entirely sure what is meant by this, though I am quite sure that the term is intended to be pejorative. It probably means applying a (medical) diagnosis and thereby implying that a (medical) treatment should follow. If that is correct then doctors do medicalise, of course, but very frequently the decision to do so has already been taken by others. Goldberg and Huxley (1980) introduced us to the idea of "filters" to specialist clinical services. If medicalisation of a problem is implied by the fact of the young person seeing a psychiatrist, then a number of people along the way need to take responsibility for that. It is not as though psychiatrists are roaming the streets in search of their patients.

What I would like to point out is that, whereas a very wide range of people could take responsibility for the medicalising of a problem, it is really only doctors who can *effectively de-medicalise*. That is to say, it is only someone with the wherewithal to make a medical diagnosis who is capable and qualified to *withhold* one. I would suggest that when doctors are enlightened and brave enough to withhold a diagnosis it will not be because no diagnosis applies. It is almost always possible to apply at least one diagnostic code. The manuals have been designed to cater for almost all eventualities with the conspicuous exception of "normality".

There may be, incumbent upon the doctor, a duty to rule out a diagnosis that might reasonably be thought to apply, particularly if it pertains to a dangerous condition, but she should hesitate before hunting down all applicable diagnoses. The raising of the question and the act of looking have their consequences, and unnecessary or unhelpful diagnoses should certainly not be imposed upon an already sufficiently satisfactory situation.

Sometimes, of course, it is essential to make a diagnosis. In medicine this can be immensely important. If someone is going to come to irreparable harm, or if there may be a condition that renders harmful a treatment I would otherwise apply, then I must know what to diagnose, know how to diagnose it, and get on with it.

But this very rarely arises in mental health. Some of the physical complications of psychoactive medications need to be quickly picked up and acted on. Any doctor reading this should know what I am talking about. It can also be important, though less precipitous, to provide a clear opinion, for example, on whether or not voices are psychotic (even if the phenomenology and nosology are uncertain), or whether the pattern of distractibility and hyperkinesis is likely to respond to stimulant medication. I shall not elaborate further, because this is where the textbooks come in, but it will already be noticeable that we are shading into issues of social construction, questions of degree, and less toxic treatment approaches that are collaborative and have less predictable outcomes. Diagnosis may be a necessary step to life-saving treatment. It can also be part of the rush to a spurious certainty. This may more often be the case in mental health work than in other areas.

I hope I am beginning to clarify why I believe that I should a) be trained in the discipline of diagnosis, but b) develop a disciplined resistance towards the invitation to diagnose. Managers and commissioners who insist on a diagnosis being recorded for everyone clearly do not understand the importance of this resistance. It is the clinician's responsibility, patiently and persistently, to educate them.

Selective attention and slavish adherence to the necessity of diagnosis, and neglect of its potential to do harm, lead us to a situation where a tabloid editor, their readership, the healthcare managers, and the patient, can believe wholeheartedly, though fallaciously, that the doctor who "fails " to make a diagnosis is either incompetent or negligent. Having said this, I do know that professional training is essential and that it imparts a great deal of useful information and skill. It is important, for example, to be aware of the very wide range of symptoms that can be associated with depressed mood. If I did not know that these can include various kinds of sleep and appetite disturbance, for example, I might make a hasty and superficial judgement about someone's mood, and underestimate the severity of the situation. This could be very dangerous. What I am saying, in a nutshell, is, "Know your stuff, but don't go nuts."

Instruments of assessment

By instruments I am not referring to objects made of stainless steel, but things like questionnaires. Like so many of the things that I call into question, they have their uses. But there is little doubt in my mind that a questionnaire comes between the clinician and the patient. To suggest that, when a clinician and a patient have only one hour together, it is a good idea to spend any of that time on the completion of a questionnaire is to grossly insult the skills of the clinician.

I should make some effort to explain what I mean by "clinician" because I am not talking here about people who are *not really working as clinicians*. If someone who has *not* been trained in taking a history, let us say, of sleep disturbance, is required to do so, she will need a list of questions.

I shall turn this story around, with a sad reflection on my own practice. We were asked (or should I say told?) to complete "outcome measures" for all patients—the more the merrier—and were given a collection of possible questionnaires to use. One of these is designed to track symptoms of depression and anxiety and includes the statement, "I am bothered by bad or silly thoughts or pictures in my mind," requiring the subject to answer either "never", "sometimes", "often", or "always". Studies may show that this instrument can be reliably used across time to track symptoms, but a number of the young people I have given the questionnaire to have questioned this item. Several have left it blank (they may be the most healthy). One wrote, "I am not a child!" (he might be slightly oppositional, though I would suggest mainly somewhat feisty). I have been asked questions in attempts to discern whether the item refers to images believed in as real (which might be hallucinations) or images known by the subject to be psychological phenomena (which might be thoughts). I have been asked whether "bothered" refers to thoughts that are simply annoying, or worrying, or that are "intrusive despite resistance" (which might suggest obsessions); whether "bad or silly" refers to their own assessment of the thoughts or the anticipated assessment of others; and whether "bad" is meant to mean evil, immoral, poor quality, etc.

These are good questions. It calls to mind a story my father told me of a scientist making regular observations of a chimpanzee through a spy-hole in the door of its cubicle. One day when he made his regular visit and put his eye to the hole he could see nothing. Only on stepping back could he make out the reflection from the eye of the chimpanzee watching him.

These questions asked of me by my patients deserve to be taken seriously, but taking them seriously a) requires some time, and, b) probably invalidates the item. The fact that, when asked, I didn't have a good answer may reveal that I have not been sufficiently trained in the use of the instrument or that I haven't given it sufficient thought beforehand. It might appear, therefore, that I either don't respect the questionnaire or that I don't sufficiently respect my patient. It is likely, also, to be evident that I am administering this questionnaire against my better judgement, which would demonstrate a lack of respect for myself, and model a defeated and victimised response, hardly likely to enhance the clinical engagement, treatment alliance, or placebo effect, or to set a good example to my patient.

The imposition across the board of specified assessment instruments risks trapping the clinician into either rebelling against their employer and risking their position, or failing their professional training and conscience. To go back to the matter of "clinician", perhaps what I mean is that people should do their job. If a person's job is to administer a series of questionnaires and carry out a manualised treatment, referring the patient on to someone else if she doesn't get better, then that is fine, but if my job is to be a psychiatrist, for example, then I should be one and do what being one entails, rather than being untaught my craft in order to do something else.

A questionnaire or assessment template may be a useful aide–mémoire but, since looking at the page instead of the patient will undermine the relationship, it comes as a poor second to memorising and becoming familiar with the questions one wants to ask. In my view, nothing replaces a well-trained clinician in intelligent engagement with his patient.

Problem saturation versus solution focus

If we were lucky we learned several things during childhood about shaping behaviour. One is that behaviour is better shaped by encouragement towards a pleasurable outcome than by the threat of an aversive one. Another is that it feels nicer to have attention drawn to success than to failure, and that noticing nice things generally makes them happen more often. Solution-focused therapies have demonstrated and used these happy facts.

A risk-avoidant strategy for mental health care, on the other hand, is liable to draw our attention constantly back to the problems and failures in our lives. This is a less efficient way of shaping positive behaviours, makes us less happy, and generally promotes a downwards spiral, creating more problems in the long run.

Therapeutic assessment

In contrast to the harmful assessment is the assessment that proves to be, or even sets out to be, of direct therapeutic benefit. Close on the heels of the ethical principal of non-maleficence is that of beneficence. I would like anything I do in connection with my patient to be of some positive benefit. This may be a slightly fanciful or idealistic position but, when it comes to first appointments, there is the possibility that this will be the only opportunity to either help the patient or create a positive enough impression of mental health services for further help to be given later. I remember being taught that the taking of a proper psychiatric history could be therapeutic to the patient. Given the theories and experience of narrative therapy, solution-focused or systemic questioning, and the integrative efforts of a good biopsychosocial formulation this should not come as a surprise. Hopefully someone will leave their own assessment less scared of the prospect of professional help, a degree of hope sustained by a new perspective on themselves and their situation, and possibly a new conversation between family members.

Healthcare services appear, despite the talk of integration, to be increasingly structured with separate stages delivered by separate elements of the service. There are call centres, triage services, and arrangements that separate assessing clinicians from those delivering therapy. Under these circumstances there is a particular necessity for that assessing clinician to serve not only as a good ambassador for the subsequent stage (not raising expectations too high, yet instilling some hope), but also as a therapeutic agent to some extent, in case the articulations of the service prove too crotchety for the patient to adhere to the process and attend for the next stage.

When it is known at the outset that the assessment will lead to further management in another part of the wider service, it can still be a rare and important opportunity to engage the young person with the idea of positive change and the potential for the CAMH service to assist them in that. In this situation positive engagement with the actual clinician doing the assessment is less what is required, and may even be counterproductive since the young person may later hark back to the promise, either actual or imagined, that was made by this first clinician, and use this to undermine their subsequent treatment. The clinician therefore may need to make it less of a personally empathic engagement and more an introduction of engaging ideas.

Ougrin, Zundel, and Ng (2009) have developed a model for therapeutic risk assessment after deliberate self-harm. The most important function of such a model should be, in my view, simply to reveal to clinicians the possibility that a therapeutic outcome might be something to aspire to in this situation. Once this attitude is struck, and provided the clinician does not try to be too personally heroic to the detriment of subsequent engagement with another part of the service, a "right approach" is likely to follow, the clinician drawing on his own therapeutic models and experience.

I will be so bold as to suggest that, by adopting an attitude of *being with* whilst working squarely within the zone of one's professional training, an assessment is likely both to be therapeutic in its own right and to serve the greater therapeutic venture of the service in its relationship with the child and family.

Clinical risk assessment

Some of the information gleaned in any assessment will be redundant when it comes to presenting it to another, and what is left out will depend on the issue at hand. It may be mainly a matter of deciding the diagnostic formulation, or it may be that treatment has got stuck somewhere and some change in direction is to be considered. In each case what is needed is the most relevant information, both positive (I do not mean merely favourable), such as, "He smokes marijuana daily," and negative, for example, "There is no history of psychotic illness in the family." We sometimes say "the positives and the important negatives" presumably because we believe that, as we have not sought unimportant information, there will be no unimportant positives to communicate.

In risk assessment the focus is on the future, in an attempt to predict and prevent serious harm to, or caused by, our patient. We have to draw the line somewhere and we do so at points along scales of proximity to our patient (we might aim to influence the drinking pattern of a parent, but not a neighbour), seriousness (deliberate self-harm, but not breaking a toy), and predictability/preventability (side effects of medication, but not catching influenza).

Future events are divided up, then, into those that cause harm to or by my patient, are reasonably predictable, and are within the sphere of influence. All the rest is discarded. There is an element of public and professional education and awareness, of course. We did not consider the risk of sexual exploitation as carefully, if at all, prior to the uncovering of its extent in recently well-publicised cases.

Then we look for evidence for each discrete risk, such as previous occurrences, stated intentions, and factors that can be expected to influence them either way. The presence or absence of important influential factors enables this exercise to be more than an attempt merely to predict the odds of each unwanted event. Once risk, protective, and resilience factors are identified for each risk there is scope for tracking across time (when the trusted grandparent dies a risk may increase; when the school exams are over one may decrease). Knowing that the risk of a specific event has increased provides an opportunity for added effort on the part of services. Knowing which factors impinge on a given risk provides possibilities for targeted intervention, such as reducing alcohol consumption or teaching social communication strategies.

I have slipped into explaining the basics, but I do so in order to now wonder, using the example of assessment after deliberate self-harm, how my suggestions in relation to assessment may apply. This example is chosen, not only because it is a common example of overt clinical risk assessment but because I have a hunch that the young people presenting in this way are increasingly turning out to be already open to the service, an observation that leads me to believe that we are failing to hold our patients and chimes with the concern that motivates the writing of this book.

As it may be a first and only clinical contact for this young person, it needs to be therapeutic in some measure as well as supportive of engagement with a service or process of change. Risk assessment is not a solution-focused exercise but a solution-focused element could easily be introduced, given that strengths are already being elicited, as one way to make it therapeutic, rather than simply fact-gathering. Ougrin and others (Ougrin et al., 2009) suggest an approach that uses the insight obtainable through a cognitive analytic therapy approach. Also, the experience of being heard as well the possibility, even tantalisingly slight, that there may be a way forwards will both engage and, to some extent, heal.

No doubt because of the spectre of suicide, this is an area in which it can be tempting to give too much place to assessment instruments, checklists, or questionnaires—the comfort objects of the service, if not of the clinician. Just when the risks dictate a need for better than average engagement, our institutional anxieties cause us to put in place mechanisms that threaten to undermine it in exchange for a dubious increase in precision.

Genuine genuineness, *being* rather than *doing* one's profession, engaging intelligently in the process of attempting an understanding, rekindling hope in the future, are all such crucial aspects of the process that it simply risks too much to spend more than the minimum time on a questionnaire. If it is demanded of the situation, perhaps it should be administered as part of the initial medical assessment or triage, so that the psychosocial assessment can include as many of these important and interpersonal components as possible.

The principle that it is difficult (or impossible) to measure something without affecting it applies. In clinical risk assessment it would be irresponsible to behave as though the assessment had no role in risk mitigation or, conversely, had no potential to increase certain important risks. In clinical practice the relationship between assessment and management is one of enmeshment. We should behave as though we know that it is impossible to separate risk assessment from clinical management. When my patient leaves the consulting room after a follow-up appointment I should be alert to the possibility that the situation they are going towards might not be a safe one for them. Not only should an assessment with a focus on risk expect to be therapeutic in some way, carried out by a clinician who is skilled in some treatment modalities as well as assessment; risk also needs to be considered within the mainstream of clinical practice. No clinician can be a "one-trick pony" if they are to be of much use.

All of this makes risk assessment very much more like *being with* someone than measuring some aspect of them. It brings into sharp focus, of course, the matter of *saying goodbye*, because that moment is quite likely to be imminent, even at the outset. If the assessing clinician will not be the one providing follow-up, then that fact needs to be stated early, and some means of contact, either with the assessing clinician or their colleagues, should be provided in the interim. Efforts should be made, as I have said, to establish and use a relationship without raising unrealistic expectations of it.

Summary

- Assessment in the clinical context begins a clinical relationship in which there is a duty of care.
- Assessment should be of need and readiness for clinical services, and the means, risks, and likely benefits of providing them.
- Clinicians may find themselves under a regrettable degree of pressure to provide labels.
- In some situations it is important to diagnose, but in others it is important *not* to do so.
- Assessment is an exercise of power; it may not be pleasant and may have negative effects. Freely informed consent should evolve throughout the process, which should be made as pleasant and constructive as possible.
- Assessment instruments may be necessary for research and to demonstrate outcomes to a third party but in clinical practice they do not replace the engaged intelligence of a good clinician.
- Special and subtle attention needs to be paid to engagement in situations where assessment and treatment are carried out by different clinicians and separated in time.

CHAPTER EIGHT

Treatment

In this book, what was the context of the treatment—the "between the lines"—has become the focus of interest and declared itself to be therapeutic. Treatment and context keep swapping places; figure becomes ground and ground, figure. In placing emphasis on the therapeutic effect of what surrounds specific treatments, I am begging the question of what I actually mean when I talk about "treatment".

The word, in both of its most common usages, reflects this ambiguity. How I treat my patient can refer to my general demeanour and attitude towards them along with things like car-parking or waiting facilities, or it can refer to my choice of first-line antipsychotic medication, and how cautious I am in making dosage changes.

This chapter gets much closer to talking about the doing aspect of things, though still focuses on what has been called by some the "non-specific" component of the treatment: not so much what to do as how to do it. I shall use specific examples of clinical situations and types of treatment in order to do so. First, though, I shall explore a little more what it is that we mean when we talk about treatment.

Treatment: figure and ground

It is important to understand what constitutes treatment, and not only for the purpose of explaining *being with*. Our patients, their parents, and their referrers might wonder when "treatment" is going to start, and our commissioners might ask us to record the time from referral to treatment and therefore be interested in the same question. I feel quite clear in my own mind that my clinical treatment of someone starts with my first face-to-face meeting with them and finishes when I say good-bye, hopefully face-to-face also but occasionally by some other medium.

Vanessa, seventeen years old, is the subject of an urgent referral to the service by her GP who is concerned that she might be suicidal. She attends with her parents. In the course of the first appointment the psychiatrist asks her if she can keep herself safe until her next appointment two or three weeks away. She agrees and everybody is reassured. Has anything changed and, if so, what?

Leaving aside the possibility that the GP might have been wrong in her assessment of urgency (and, for the sake of argument, I shall say that on this occasion she wasn't) let us think about what happened, and how. During the course of the consultation the psychiatrist's own anxiety and understanding of the risk Vanessa posed became more nuanced and better informed. Over the same period Vanessa's own distress reduced and her parents became less anxious than they were at the outset. Were these connected? Had a genuine reduction in risk been achieved or was it an illusion? Had the psychiatrist simply convinced herself that the risk was or had become less than everyone had thought, and was her conviction contagious? Was the establishment of a relationship genuinely protective? To what extent was this trick, and to what extent treatment? Was the reduction of anxiety an encouraging sign of engagement with life, or was it the main purpose of this early intervention? How much was the psychiatrist's confidence genuine, and how much was it constructed out of necessity? These are rhetorical questions. The answer is along the lines of, "all of the above".

We can distinguish Vanessa's despair from her depression. We know that it would be unlikely for any depressive illness to be treated in that short space of time. Treating her depression, treating her distress, treating *her*, and treating the system are none of them quite the same thing. Whether this vignette is an instance of therapeutic assessment or of treatment starting at the first appointment depends on what happens subsequently.

> Zac had been my patient for a number of years. His mother was an addict at the time of his birth and he was brought up by an aunt. He was someone whose manner suggested a mild degree of autism, but his history suggested attachment problems. He also showed behaviour that satisfied the criteria for a diagnosis of attention deficit hyperactivity disorder. After a couple of years of advice to the school, behavioural support and attempts to engage him in a talking therapy, his aunt, who had hitherto resisted the idea of medication, changed her mind as his school placement was under threat. First-line medication seemed to help his attention, but was accompanied by sudden oppositional rages. As he left after an appointment in which I had discussed a second-line medication, explaining the risks, he said, "Thank you for trying to help me Dr West," prompting astonished, grateful, and affectionate remonstrations from his aunt towards him. As it happened, the second-line medication appeared responsible for unusual neurological symptoms and bizarre behaviour, and also had to be stopped. We carried on "trying to help" with further conversations and further medications.

As a treatment, the first two medications in this case could not be regarded as a success. If the aim of treatment was to bring about a reduction in behavioural problems and a secure educational placement, we could certainly not yet relax in the knowledge that we had achieved our aim. And yet, for this young man, "trying to help" was something worth thanking me for.

What we see in Vanessa's case is something, regarded ostensibly as the main symptom, reduced without any specific treatment having taken place. In the second example what some might describe as a string of failed treatments was nevertheless experienced by Zac as something of positive value. Interventions that we have given the signifier "treatment" can be harmful. Other things, considered not to be treatments, or to be failed treatments, can turn out to be therapeutic.

Listening, valuing, encouraging a narrative, alerting people to multiple truths, shifting the emphasis, or changing the agenda, can all be therapeutic, and so could be argued to be treatment. I shall suggest that simply buying time for the child can often be the most therapeutic thing we do, even whilst carrying out relatively useless complex actions called "treatments".

Treatment, therefore, is not exactly the same as therapy, and neither of them has a monopoly on, or even a reliable relationship with, being therapeutic.

A further note on figure and ground

The child is within nested contexts, each of which can be figure or ground, depending on the perspective. Starting with society as ground, the figure might be the family, which is the ground for the child, who, along with the family and the wider context, becomes the ground for the issue-described-as-problem. I am playing with words, and hope that, in doing so, I can convey something of importance.

The referral of the child to the service starts the treatment episode. How we treat the child and his family can be divided into non-specific aspects which are themselves figure on the ground of the episode (waiting room, promptness, the wording of letters, warmth, etc.) but which, taken as an ensemble, become the ground on which specific treatments take place.

We hope that aspects of the non-specific treatment might be therapeutic. We certainly hope that the specific treatment will be. I take it as axiomatic that, in order for the specific treatment to be therapeutic it needs to take place within a therapeutic relationship. This is a specific relationship between the professional and the child, primarily, but also their family. The therapeutic relationship should be entered into deliberately, rather than by accident, and it should have certain attributes. This is as good a point as any to point out that the shift of language from therapeutic relationship towards treatment episode underscores the fact that the interaction framing treatment is more between a patient and the service, than an individual clinician within the service.

The specific complex behaviours intended to be the main therapeutic intervention can be called therapies. They may be behavioural, cognitive-behavioural, group, family/systemic, pharmacological, etc., or they can be slightly confusingly one of a group of therapeutic approaches called "psychotherapy". These are generally informed by psychodynamic principles which, in turn, find their origins roughly speaking in the Freudian revolution. They pay attention to—exploit, navigate—unconscious process and the comparative and symbolic relationships between aspects of the therapeutic relationship itself, overt problem in the outside world, and historic primal relationships with key attachment figures, the three corners of what Malan called the "triangle of person" (1979, pp. 80, 92–94).

The single most important point I want to make out of all of this is that, because we do not know which of the "figure" and the "ground" is going to prove the more therapeutic (or destructive) we must pay attention to, and bring our professional training and experience to bear on, both.

Anyone who places me in a context with the expectation that I do "treatment" must be prepared for me to show an active and professional interest in the context in which they have placed me.

The meaning of treatment

One powerful meaning of treatment, particularly in tablet form, is likely to be that there is something missing or wrong in the child and that he needs something not normally accessible to him. It is, in short, a rather disempowering and invalidating construct. These are side effects of the treatment not listed in the formulary or product information. Just as we acknowledge the existence of non-specific therapeutic effects, so we might regard these meanings as non-specific side effects of treatment.

Parenting programmes teach parents to encourage positive behaviours rather than attacking and attempting to eradicate negative ones. This is based on the behavioural discovery that reward is a more effective reinforcer than is punishment. This may be partly because it is impossible to engage in no behaviour at all, and the modelling and encouragement of a behaviour therefore fills the vacuum left by the unwanted behaviour as it leaves. If unfilled, this vacuum simply draws the negative behaviour straight back into its old place. We also know that negative attention is more rewarding than no attention. There are all sorts of reasons for saying that to change behaviour one should reinforce the wanted, rather than focus and lavish attention on the unwanted.

Yet we do the opposite in much of our clinical practice. We ask for, look for, investigate, to uncover what were previously covert signs of the unwanted, and then we concentrate our efforts on eliminating it, inviting the patient back to follow-up appointments where they will be asked if the unwanted has gone yet. The dynamics of treatment can too easily slip into those of hate and fear. The parents may believe that they do not hate or fear their child, but the same may not be clear to the child. Parents will use expressions like, "He was really good last week," meaning that he caused his parents little worry. They are partly looking forward to being able to forget about him. Needless to say, it is important that the child does not feel hated or feared.

Treatment, then, should not be pushed upon the patient prematurely. There must be sufficient understanding of what it means to the patient and those around them. There must be sufficient permission given to retain the symptom, provided it does not present an acute and real threat. Time must be given to allow the symptom and the child to acknowledge each other's independent validity and to move apart. There must be sufficient, by way of alternative, to fill the space.

I would prefer, if at all possible, to validate both the parent and child perspective and suggest that each has what it takes to get through life, and each may be held back in their own unique way. This is best done by insinuation, by paying attention to each narrative and maintaining the assumption that their perspectives and respective needs are valid and compatible. There are elements of approaches described elsewhere that work towards this stance. Values-based practice is one that is yet to be properly described and disseminated, but the social construction lens and narrative-based therapeutic approaches of family-systemic therapy are well-established examples of how one might elicit and explore the meaning of treatment, improving choices of treatment direction, adherence, or bringing about resolution without any other treatment being needed. Indeed, the proper obtaining of informed consent would be another.

Cognitive behavioural therapy might argue, also, that it explores the thoughts and assumptions (schemas, values) of the patient and that if these are properly taken into account the therapy will not do violence to the patient or their world view. I suspect that, practised properly, most mainstream therapies, and very probably most complementary therapies, enshrine these principles in one way or another. The trick is in remembering this when one is in the room.

The meaning of illness

It is impossible to grasp the meaning of treatment without understanding the meaning of symptoms and illness to the patient.

> Gemma, aged fifteen, was seen within the paediatric clinic because of chest pains, palpitations, and collapse. Investigation returned results that reassured the doctor and to some extent the mother, but not Gemma herself, and I was asked to see her. I did this in a joint clinic with the paediatrician, rather than in my own clinic, because I was not convinced that, for

her, the meaning of the symptoms had shifted enough for a change in the investigative and therapeutic focus to be acceptable. Whilst giving this time to change, there was work to be done fending off "educational welfare" (which could be roughly translated as "whether or not to take the mother to court"). Other agencies also needed help with their own impoverished understanding, thus far focused on whether these symptoms meant "illness", meriting pity and a free pass, or "malingering", in which case either the child or the parent is bad and deserves punishment. At this point the balance of therapeutic focus could safely swing towards Gemma and her mother where it stayed for a dozen or so sessions of conjoint work that I shared with a therapist and spaced over a year and a half. At discharge her pain was very rare but, more significantly, she confidently told us that when she did feel chest pain she knew it meant that she was either worrying about or angry with her father.

In this story pain, at the outset, meant illness, normal investigative results meant malingering, and the (paternal?) statutory services were persecutory. By the end, pain had come to represent, for Gemma, the vulnerability of the previously persecutory father who, like the statutory services, could now be tolerated.

Stephen, who had been treated intermittently over several years for a life-threatening illness, was referred because his mood dropped during episodes of treatment with a medication that is known for behavioural and affective side effects. A predecessor had already started him on antidepressants and there was little to do other than evolve a ritual of minor adjustments of his antidepressant dose at these times with reminders that each treatment was fairly brief. When he went into long-term remission and was discharged from the paediatric team, everyone, not least he, was dismayed to find he was still depressed—possibly even more so than before. He had earlier depicted his illness as a very powerful (male) monster and he experienced dismay bordering at times on panic at the departure of this organising principle. His (single) mother and he formed a courageous dyad. I could not help thinking of his illness as a rather cruel, but thus-far predictable, parent, and reflected with them on how it might have been more than an attentive and competent paediatric team that they had lost.

As a friend of mine was told by the driver of a bus when she discovered it was not, as she had believed, going to Cork after all, "You should never presume a thing." It would be, and often is, too easy to presume that the presenting symptom is the problem, and its removal is the solution. It can be important not to remove the symptom prematurely. If it made some aspect of the world safe, or gave the child some sort of voice, it is important, first, to secure those achievements by other means.

Un-therapeutic treatment

In the previous chapter, the story of Sameenah was given as an instance of untherapeutic assessment, but it could also figure here. None of what passed was a disaster and, indeed, treatment disasters are not what I am referring to here. It is a story of a treatment episode fractured by the disjointed configuration of the service. This disempowered Sameenah's clinicians and the treatment, introducing fruitless periods of inaction. The system was incapable of responding, as an individual or close-knit team would have done, to her request that further scrutiny and questionnaires be avoided, and it was unable to introduce elements of specialised anxiety treatment, which remained tantalisingly out of reach. The process was impersonal, insensitive, and ineffectual. When skilled treatment for anxiety came closest, it did so as an unwelcome and useless intrusion—as a negative figure on the ground of an emasculated treatment episode. The situation was redeemed by flipping this configuration over and understanding specialist anxiety clinics as part of the problematic ground against which an ongoing therapeutic relationship could figure. The psychiatrist was able to situate himself beside her and together they were able to talk about specialist clinics as *things* like schools, families, examination rooms, and bus stops, which she encountered and mastered in life.

Waiting lists, in general, are negative and un-therapeutic. The solution-focused process goes on hold and instead a period of unsupported rumination on the symptom ensues. The belief that you need something and are not getting it, and the experience of seeing others go before you, do not boost confidence. As Adam Phillips has pointed out, it is particularly difficult to appreciate something for which you have waited too long (Phillips, 1994, p. 55).

The treatment episode begins at the point that the service accepts the referral, and long waits, impersonal communication missing its mark, etc. all become ways that the service treats the patient, and are subtle forms of emotional abuse and neglect. The patient is often in a therapeutic relationship with the referrer already. She might have been better off staying in that relationship than abandoning it, or being abandoned by it, in favour of a neglectful and insensitive one. This applies to all ailments, mild or serious. If something needs to be done, it usually needs to be done now. If not, then you can be told to get on with life, but that is likely to be easier to do if someone sticks around for a bit in case they are needed.

Long waits, interrogations that do not require effort on the part of the interrogator, and off the peg treatments all carry meanings which will be slightly different for each person but are unlikely to include, "I am valued as an individual and of importance to the world which wants to understand me and help me."

Conroy had been maltreated by his parents at a very young age and placed in a series of temporary fostering arrangements before he was adopted into a family who found themselves barely able to contain his disturbed behaviour. They did so, however, with very little therapeutic support. He was someone who failed to fall squarely into a convenient diagnostic grouping of either attachment failure or neurodevelopmental disturbance, showing "features" of pretty much everything including, at times, disturbance of thinking and perception that suggested a psychotic process. One evening he was apprehended by the police in a disturbed state and admitted to the adult psychiatric ward as there was no adolescent bed available. The on-call child and adolescent psychiatrist was telephoned in the early hours of the morning by a flummoxed junior doctor who reported that despite two different antipsychotic medications and a minor tranquiliser, Conroy's behaviour seemed to be becoming more disturbed. The consultant's intervention was to recommend Conroy be given less medication rather than more, and Conroy settled over the next twenty-four hours and was able to be discharged home again a couple of days later.

Needless to say, this was not, the end of Conroy's troubles, and his story is one of both figure and ground failures, but this brief glimpse serves to illustrate the fact that people are complex and that simple medical interventions can make matters worse instead of better, particularly when fundamental background issues are not being addressed.

A friend in a high-ranking position within the charitable (indeed, humanitarian) sector had been required, with his department, to attend a team-building function. He later described at a dinner party and to general hilarity the attempts of the group facilitator to persuade him to say, about himself and colleagues, things that he did not want to say and almost certainly did not believe. He was a fairly robust individual and was able to smile down the assault, but it required effort and the deployment of his very considerable social and self-calming skills to do so, and he was shocked.

In the middle of last century there flourished a number of group approaches designed to achieve subjective and behavioural change in people. Like any approach favoured because of the speed of its effect, they ran the risk of cutting corners and becoming brutal. Individuals can be induced to be cruel to other individuals under a variety of pressures. Famous and disturbing experiments by Milgram (electric shock) and Zimbardo (Stanford "prison") in the sixties and seventies, respectively, showed us how far people can be induced by setting and instruction, but we have most of us seen milder forms of cruelty arising spontaneously in the school playground and sometimes in the workplace. Happily, children can be socialised out of bullying. What we forget is how easily adults can be socialised back into it. As we are intelligent and provided we are not at war, we ought to have less sympathy with the practice of lambasting someone as repressed or arrogant because of their reluctance to similarly lambast others. Yet the T-group approach appears still to thrive in the corporate world, and may be expected to spread into healthcare, given the inroads that business methods are making into that sector.

A medical student in his mid twenties, who was later to write a book on therapeutic attitude, was in a psychodrama group. His relative social reticence resulted in his being, in the last hour of a weekend workshop, one of only two who had not so far volunteered themselves as protagonist. Not wanting this to be forever the case, he stepped forwards. Half an hour later the entire group was furiously stamping on cushions in an admirably cohesive attempt to support him in the eradication of an aspect of his personality; it might have been his reticence. It took him the best part of a year to regain his composure, and another thirty years to learn to practice self-compassion.

I don't know if the group facilitator reflected on the session or remembers it still but, were I in their shoes, I would hope to notice the self-critical dynamic and find a way to draw the session to a close, perhaps with some two-chair work in which the protagonist could use the resources he had (one "part" of himself to help the other) to make some sort of compassionate commitment to himself. Or I might have invited the group to offer appreciative or supportive suggestions that could acknowledge his discomfort and his wish to change, distinguishing the unwanted behaviour from the wanting self.

I offer these vignettes to make the point that powerful therapeutic techniques abound, and that well-meaning therapists can fail in the therapeutic endeavour. The therapist's or facilitator's belief in the method is necessary, but there is a risk that it may invite their collusion with the haste, and the wish to eradicate the bad, that generally prevails in these sorts of situation.

Not treating

Much of what I have written in other chapters has been about how to not act. This is not the same as doing nothing. Nor is it to be regarded as either lazy or easy. In a therapeutic context, not acting can be exhausting. To responsibly and safely not act requires experience and skill. Using both senses of the word, sometimes the best way to treat someone is to not treat them. Experience and a relationship with the patient is needed in order to know when this is the case.

The employment of time in the patient's interest

Time is required for the growth of understanding and the finding of a voice, the catching up of a developmental delay, or the adjustment of parental expectations. It involves getting the pressing agenda of the adult world off the child's back. The child can take stock, notice some alternatives, and resume the project of becoming herself. Françoise Dolto, coined the term *allant-devenant*, which proves difficult to translate but calls to mind something along the lines of going-on-becoming or continuing-to-become. (For three translations of *allant-devenant* into English, see Hall, Hivernel & Morgan, 2009, pp. 34, 90, 161). It no doubt bears a relationship to Winnicott's "going on being" (Ogden, 2004) but, where Winnicott was referring to a maternal continuity-function, *allant-devenant* conveys to me more of a flavour of a person's ongoing individual developmental project. From a psychoanalytic perspective, I have no doubt it seems at its most startling and rapid in infancy, but I believe that it continues throughout our lives becoming particularly conscious, radical, and challenging through adolescence partly because the environs fight back.

People do not generally go to the doctor in order for nothing to be done, particularly if they have been encouraged up to this point in the belief that there is something wrong. But some tasks are sufficiently engrossing and important that they require the distractions around them to pause. *Allant-devenant* would at times be one. Yet the world is generally not very good at pausing. A sufficiently powerful person, or a person with a sufficiently powerful agenda, is required to make it possible. Doctors and treatments still wield this kind of power. The world will stop while a doctor or nurse is taking the pulse and whilst a treatment takes place. This is the sickness role in action. It is dangerous, though, if the only way we can get the world to pause and allow our development, is through becoming sick. It is dangerous because maintaining the pause—maintaining the sickness—becomes the project instead of the development that it was supposedly enabling. The clinician, therefore, has to find a way of permitting something like the sick role, whilst minimising the requirement for actual sickness.

If one is to buy time for the child it is important that the situation is, and is seen to be, held by a capable pair of hands. This would be an example of art, not mimicking reality, but creating it. A powerful person creates the impression of taking matters into their hands and, by doing so, is able to slow time down and actually enable treatment to take place. The treatment is often an actual clinical treatment, but it could be simply the holding still—the psychological equivalent of a plaster cast—that enables the self-healing developmental process to take place.

I do have considerable faith in the homeostatic and health-seeking capacity of the living organism, and I am inclined to the view that, if the damaging process is stopped and the child has enough in place in the way of emotional and personal support, he will recover and resume something close to his inherent or optimal developmental trajectory. Broadly speaking, I am in favour of the minimum intervention to achieve this—always accepting that the minimum intervention needs, on occasion, to be utterly drastic.

As well as being minimal, treatment requires a time course. This flows on as a necessity from what I have said about such things as understanding the meaning of the presentation, problems, potential treatment, as well as sensitivity as to timing, feedback and, when it comes to it, saying goodbye. There is a trajectory to treatment that I compare to the arc of a thrown ball, or that of a dive. Design engineers are taught the mathematical properties of aesthetic curves, but these designs work because they match an aesthetic instinct that we all have. It does not take much in the way of aesthetic sensibility to discern the correct curve of a thrown ball or a dive. There are determinants of how far, high, or deep we can go, and there are dangers to getting it wrong. If an aeroplane runs out of fuel before it has landed it crashes to the ground. If a diver stays down too long, or rises to fast, she suffocates or suffers decompression sickness.

Surface for breath

But I shall allow "reality to intrude". The rest of this chapter will adopt the convention that certain discrete activities are treatments, in a way that everything else that happens around them is not.

Treatments, then, for the rest of this chapter, will be things like cognitive behavioural therapy; psychoeducation; parenting programmes; behaviour therapy; family systemic therapy; psychodynamically informed individual and group psychotherapy (verbal and nonverbal); and pharmacotherapy such as stimulants, antidepressants, and antipsychotics. This is not an exhaustive list, but it is enough a) to make the point that in general parlance treatments are the figure and not the ground, and b) to provide sufficient examples with which to explore how one might maintain a therapeutic attitude whilst treating someone.

Informing and supporting parents

If parents are functioning sufficiently well as parents—if, in Winnicott's terms, they are *good enough* parents (this absolutely requiring them to be *inter alia* not *too* good)—they will be the most important therapists, and it may well be that no other specific treatment will be required.

On the other hand, if they are *bad* enough, then no amount of therapy for the child in the here and now will help very much, although it may help if he has been responded to with respect by someone who has faith in his capacity and right to become a viable human individual. Memories of positive relationships, however fleeting, can enable hope and can sustain us through a dangerous wilderness. The possibility of therapy and/or development towards health may be drawn upon later, when the noxious influence is dimmed.

There are undoubtedly times when children need to be protected from their parents but this is rarely considered to be in the province of clinical treatment. More relevant, here, would be the idea of supporting parents to be *good enough*. This might involve giving the parents useful information and advice. If assessment of the child and the parents shows this to be necessary and possible, I would consider it to be a first-line treatment after hearing the child: hear the child and support the parents. The latter need not be provided in the same setting, though for reasons given in Chapter Six I think there is value in the child seeing that the same clinician or group of clinicians can understand and relate to them and their parents at the same time.

Parents can be supported in any number of ways. Empathy, understanding, and compassion are all essential. Parents are humans almost invariably doing the best they can. The social service family centres used to provide a mug of tea with toast and Marmite, along with some space and time, someone to talk to if necessary, and often something resembling play therapy for the child. One of the beauties of this approach was that it could achieve quite a lot in a low-key way, sought out by the parent who retained a degree of agency, all the time effectively allowing an ongoing safeguarding assessment to take place.

If it feels like gaining access to resources, that is fine, but what is the likely meaning to the parents of being given parental advice or parent training? I do remember what it was like to be a parent. If the Englishman's home is his castle, then his approach to parenting is his sovereignty. Being advised to attend a parenting programme is likely to carry the meaning that one is not good enough. Being told that the advice is consistent with national guidance, or is generic, is unlikely to help much. It might simply add an officious insult to the narcissistic injury.

Clinicians will do what they can to manage this situation. I have found it often works if the parents and I, once alongside one another, collectively agree that parenting is the job that we are not trained for, but are thrown into at the deep end—that "we all do our best; that is what parent's do". It is usually acceptable to suggest that in some situations generic parenting skills are not enough and expert parent skills are needed, though the implication that they have a problem child should be avoided, however appealing that idea might be to the parents. This is another tightrope, but may often be successfully walked by the device of labelling the situation rather than the child and observing that parents and child are facing it together.

I now have the advantage of age in that I am a plausible parent myself. I do not have framed photos of beaming children on the desk and generally think this inappropriate. What I do have is a sufficiently careworn look on my own face to suggest that I have failed at something I wanted to succeed at. My patients' parents do not need to know whether that was parenting, an academic career, or something else. I think that this amounts to "being with" the parents. It is a compassionate stance, alongside both parent and child.

If I can hit the right tone, then, in the role of pilot familiar with the treacherous waters, I am usually invited aboard. I can then offer enthusiastic and authoritative fine-grain advice on behavioural approaches. I have found parents invariably appreciative of the golden rules of behavioural reinforcement (fast, relevant, affordable, agreed, irreversible rewards for a very small number of specified and achievable behaviours) and the golden rule of removal of privilege (the route to getting it back must be similarly visible, specified, plausible, clear, and achievable). They are also intrigued to hear of pitfalls, including the inadvertent rewarding of unwanted behaviours or punishment of wanted ones.

It is generally true that, whatever the situation, these parenting skills will be more helpful than otherwise, though there will be times when the child and family diagnosis or predicament will demand specific treatment approaches or expert behavioural analysis.

At the other extreme—let us say when a young person is so acutely unwell that she needs an inpatient bed (at the time of writing, famously hard to come by)—I fairly easily find myself "alongside" the parents as, in that situation, I am generally half out of my own depth, not because of the psychiatry involved, but the bureaucracy and logistics.

Finally, there are some parents so disorganised, depressed, distracted, demanding, destructive, etc., that they cannot be advised or supported. The nautical analogy might be a ship without a captain, rudder, or engine, or a pirate ship. When the pilot steps on board such a vessel, they find they can hardly ever help, and they might even be placing themselves and any passengers in further danger. The thing to do is to notify the coastguards, call up a tugboat or alert the maritime police. Something more like family therapy, specific treatment for the parents, or safeguarding interventions may be necessary.

Behaviour therapy

Sam, a ten-year-old boy, was brought to the service in which I was completing my specialist training. He had a fear of needles, and there was a requirement, gradually becoming more urgent, for him to have some blood tests. His parents were anxious and I was working with a psychologist in order to learn cognitive-behavioural approaches. Over several weeks we taught him relaxation techniques and showed him photographs of hypodermic syringes. The work seemed to us to be progressing unbearably slowly and he remained painstakingly anxious until the sixth session in which he showed what seemed to be irritation. It dawned on us that he might have become the impatient, and we the more hesitant, party. We put this to him; he agreed and had his blood tests a short while later.

At what point did the anxiety about moving forwards become an impatience to do so? At the outset one small person was holding out against the anxious pushes and pulls of parents and professionals. The image comes to mind of a tug of war with a child on one end of the rope and a dozen adults on the other. At some point the child lets go of the rope and walks towards the adults. The trick, for the adults, is to get up off the floor quickly; for the parents to accompany the child further and the therapists to bow out gracefully and get on to their next patient.

In Sam's case it seems that responsibility was handed on like the baton in a relay race, accruing confidence along the way. Sam could play with the anxiety once it was no longer embodied between needle and skin and acted out between his parents and himself but was, instead, spread through different people and no doubt more workable as a consequence. He did not pick up the baton until he was well and truly ready, but then made a very convincing run to the finish line.

The case I would make for *being with* and *saying goodbye*, in this instance, would be that the timing was Sam's. The clinicians were a) there, b) with sufficient constancy and therefore, c) available at the critical moment, d) demonstrating a useful combination of interest, experience, optimism, doubt, and opportunism. The behavioural techniques no doubt also had a role to play, as did the fact that we were presented to the family and endorsed by an organisation with gravitas and panache, contributing to the stock of confidence that we all drew on.

The treatment of tics

Tics are sudden stereotyped movements. They are involuntary but can typically be resisted to some extent. They can involve different muscle groups around the body and can include the production of sounds or words. They are very common and typically emerge in middle childhood, especially in boys. They are almost always harmless unless they attract disapproval, criticism, or derision. Often parents are worried about tics, believing them to be a harbinger of something more dangerous or sinister, and they often express this anxiety in the form of pointing out to their child when the tics happen and trying to dissuade him from ticcing, believing this to be a way to make him stop. (Notice that, when the parent erroneously fears the tic to be a symptom of brain disease, their implicit magical belief is that if they or the child can instruct the symptom to go away, the brain disease will have never existed.) This raises tensions and anxiety, erodes self-esteem, and makes the tics worse.

The single most useful intervention with tics, in my view, is to explain their harmless nature and the importance of ignoring them, sometimes, and after negotiation with the child, extending this advice to the school. I also tell families that the child will very probably grow out of them, but that tics are likely to come and go in the meantime. In the event of them persisting or worsening, I say, it can be helpful to ask for a separate room when it gets to school exams, and there are a couple of medications which, while they do not usually make the tics go away completely, can often reduce their severity for a time if needed. There is a specific behavioural technique described for the treatment of tics but I have never been able to use it to any satisfactory degree.

Thomas, at thirteen, had a facial tic that was a sort of nod, and a tic of his left arm that he suppressed by holding and stroking the left wrist with his right hand. At a school meeting that I was attending, he was visibly ticcing as his teacher said, "We haven't really seen any tics at school." Because the boy was beginning to be suspected by the school to be a bit of a skiver, I thought it appropriate to point out the almost continuous tics of his writing hand. The teacher was suitably impressed and the boy was pleased and relieved. Several months later, he was receiving CBT for his social anxiety (no one available felt confident enough to deliver habit reversal). One of his beliefs was that people would see his tics and think him weird. The family were becoming slightly disgruntled that he wasn't receiving "any treatment for his tics". The question is, which of the things done at this stage could be regarded as treatment for his tics? Would CBT for social anxiety be part of the treatment of his tics, or vice versa? Over the next year or so several medications were tried with partial success and another referral was made to the psychology department. At the time of writing, Thomas's school attendance is no longer an issue and his tics are less obvious and can often be ignored. He is busy revising for exams and there is an open offer for review in my clinic.

The "rival" GP in the small town that I grew up in had a blinking tic that affected both sides but the left much more than the right, such that she was effectively winking much of the time. She would pass in the street and appear to wink at me. My fear of her was hardly to do with her tic at all. It was much more to do with her age and my sense that she had something over my mother, or perhaps vice versa. It was a child's awe at the mysteries of the adult world. I don't think that children will often bully a tic in someone that they wouldn't have bullied for something else, had the tic not been there. In my view, if a child is teased for his tics it is a mark of the quality of his friendships and of the culture of the school, rather than the severity of the tics.

> Phil returned to see me shortly before his eighteenth birthday. I had seen him from time to time since his early teens, and we had at times resorted to a very low dose of medication to relieve him of some of the burden of holding his tics back. It had had its place. When I saw him on this last occasion he was cheerful and happy in his life. He was ticcing with his head and neck quite a bit but had decided not to continue with the medication because it made him feel a bit drowsy. He had a part-time job and had an interview the next day, which he was quite confident about.

I cite the treatment of tics as an example of medication being at its most useful when not being used. The possibility of its use at some theoretical point in the future makes the tics more bearable. How many situations can be tolerated provided there is a plausible escape route?

Having said this, I do prescribe at times and will do so at minimum doses and will fiddle around with the timing or small increments of dosage. I don't know if I have just been extraordinarily lucky, but I have never had to resort to higher dosage or multiple medications. I am inclined to think that leaping to medication early has an undermining effect, disempowering the child and the family, confirming in people's minds that this is something that must, at all counts, be treated (which is clearly not the case). The belief that it is a condition that must be treated is not far from believing it must be eradicated and therefore substantially increases the risk of using heroic measures in order to achieve the impossible (and unnecessary). Managing fear and expectation is an important part of "treating" tics, along with helping families re-sort their priorities and discover self-esteem.

To do this, one has to accompany the child and family. Few people can be told something once and it will stay with them. Even less so when they enter the enchanted forest. Little Red Riding Hood was given good advice by her mother and, if her mother had stayed with her, there would have been no problem resisting the wiles of the wolf. One cannot, therefore, say all this and discharge the patient. Those who believe human behaviour is ruled by rationale will say that a leaflet can be taken away, but I expect Red Riding Hood would have pushed a leaflet into that basket where it would quickly be forgotten, buried in forest produce. Mere information cannot replace an experienced companion, eye contact, ready access, repeated messages, and encouragement. All have a cogency derived from the continued personal investment of another. No thing quite replaces them.

The treatment of psychosis

In a very different area of psychiatry, we know that antipsychotic medication, whilst it may have an important place in the treatment of psychosis, is not the only useful intervention and is certainly not a panacea. Reducing the level of expressed negative emotion in the home environment is important, as can be the identification of behavioural and cognitive strategies to reduce symptoms or their impact, and effective management of practical issues like sleep, time, learning, and life planning.

The enthusiasm for the early use of antipsychotic medication, even before psychosis is confirmed, has now somewhat dimmed. More mature reflection on the published evidence suggests that, whilst early engagement is important, the overall benefit of early use of medication is unclear, tempered by the knowledge that these medications can have serious, unpredictable, and long-term side effects (National Collaborating Centre for Mental Health, 2013).

Much as it might be nice to feel certain in situations like this, it may be more responsible to be a little circumspect, and to travel with the patient, rather than responding to one aspect of their situation with the full force of fashionable practice. This requires the clinician to wield a different sort of responsibility. The skill required for the responsible wielding of not knowing is different to that required for the responsible use of knowledge. Somehow we have to wield them both at the same time.

The "force of fashionable practice", as I have called it, presents dangers for the clinician as well as for the patient. Hypothetical—even actual—vindication in the future provides scant defence in the face of a fitness to practice panel that is fully convinced by current state of published opinion.

My fear of actively causing harm may contribute to excessive caution at times. The occasions when a deterioration in my patient have caused me to wonder if this is the case are roughly balanced by instances of which Conroy was an example in the vignette above. To some extent, and through the lens of *being with*, the uncertainty of the so-called knowledge base is something that my patient and I could be seen to be negotiating together. I am still in a position of relative power and responsibility. My own mental state is not the one under the most concerning attack, for a start. Nevertheless, I feel some degree of anxiety and obtain comfort from the notion of the experienced mountain guide, no doubt quite anxious as the storm clouds gather and landmarks become obscured, but still the one with the expertise and more likely than not to discern a successful route off the mountain.

One of the benefits of working in a large service is that I am amongst colleagues whose levels of experience are diverse and complement one another. I can consult and refer to them. *Being with* is expressed in the form of keeping in touch and being there to catch the patient when they return from, or slip out of, the specialist clinic. I retain ownership of the referral and therefore, to some extent, what happens as a consequence of it.

When a treatment or opinion is delivered by another professional I prefer there to be a visible and real relationship between us. This enables the integration of treatment or opinion into the story of that treatment episode. The professional relationship is likely to be noticed and, whether it is a hierarchical one in which I may be either parent or child to my colleague, or a more spousal one, it will model real-life relationships for the patient and so is better conducted along functional lines than otherwise. As well as being therapeutic, this can contribute to the development and maintenance of professional practice, as I shall outline in the Epilogue.

My caution in relation to medication is a good illustration of not rushing into action on a reflex. And the analogy of the reflex is apposite. When eliciting reflexes—let us say tapping below the patella with a rubber hammer—one often finds that it is not so easy. It may be that one is missing the tendon, of course, but I was taught to reinforce the reflex. This is done by asking the person to tense some pairs of complementary muscle groups. For example, they might hook the fingers of left and right hands and attempt to pull the hands apart whilst keeping them linked. Doing so results in a more vigorous reflex. In the same way, when clinicians and teams are under pressure, particularly, perhaps, the contradictory and conflicting pressures that any clinician would recognise these days, they are more likely to act on reflex. It may be in order to save precious time, or it may be because their reactive hormones are running high, or through some other process or preparedness. If there is a commissioning or political focus on the time between referral and "treatment", an intervention may be started, not because it is the right treatment or the optimum time, but because it is *a* treatment within the target time. The effect of the treatment is likely to be reduced by this mistiming and misguiding, but worse damage may be done through the effective undermining of resources inherent in the patient and family, and the inflammation of anxiety. In addition, a treatment resource may be taken away from someone who was exactly ready for it.

Treatment where knowledge does not help

It is not always helpful to know things, and it can often be very helpful to be used to not knowing. In situations where expectations are frustrated it is often the adults who are most at sea, though the child can be caught by the waves thrown up by them as they thrash around.

Eddie was diagnosed early on with a condition that gave him a life expectancy of less than two decades. He did surprisingly well and was referred to CAMHS at a stage where he was significantly disabled but was, essentially, negotiating adolescence. His parents' expectations were doubly confounded by his dying instead of growing up, and then, when they were accommodating to this, his growing up instead of dying. Everyone "knew" the prognosis. The psychiatrist "knew" that the problem was grief (but it wasn't). Over about eight mixed individual and family sessions, spanning a couple of years, some sort of understanding emerged and discharge felt right.

The child or adolescent is often better equipped to cope in this situation than the adults, despite the general consensus that the illness is happening to him. He has neither the rigid expectations of the adults, nor the tottering edifice that is threatened when its foundations are rearranged. What is more, he has a more flexible notion of time. Eddie had no psychiatric illness. The family were in some sort of struggle, and he had an adolescence to negotiate. The only criteria for being seen were the request of the referrer and the distress and compliance of the family.

Psychodynamic and systemic considerations

A psychotherapy should have a beginning and end, and should follow a framework, preferably with supervision within the same framework. Psychotherapy is a particular and specialised form of therapeutic relationship, whereas a therapeutic relationship can crop up anywhere, even fleetingly. They have in common the lodging of professional responsibility in one party.

Less need be said about *being with* in actual psychotherapy because it is largely the relative lack of psychodynamic and systemic understanding in the wider services that leads to the problem that *being with* is intended to redress. However, these, like any other treatment, are situated in a context, and something does need to be said about psychodynamic and systemic considerations outside of actual therapy.

Anyone taking responsibility for a therapeutic relationship will do so more effectively if they understand something of the psychotherapies. Those who work in mental health services, particularly at a senior level where they are likely to be providing supervision and consultative opinions to others, need at least a modicum of training in psychodynamic process, including a familiarity with such concepts as unconscious motivation, transference, splitting, denial, and projection. They also need some understanding of behavioural and cognitive behavioural cause and effect, as well as the systemic processes and patterns that so often confound them. These processes will be in operation within the team as well as within the patient system.

A little knowledge can be a dangerous thing. Whilst "a modicum of training" in the therapies is required for all senior clinicians, it is also very important for all mental health clinicians to have ready access to a high level of psychotherapeutic expertise. For this reason, mental health work of any complexity should be done in multidisciplinary teams in which individual team members contribute to a range of expertise including these psychotherapies. In this way the expertise is available to all, the work is done in an ambiance that understands and uses it, and fully skilled treatments are available in a sufficiently wide range of modalities.

In order to be of use in the most troubling of situations, we need to be able to stop ourselves from plunging in, encouraging regressions and dismantling defences, in those situations where to do so might be particularly explosive or erosive to the patient or their system. We need to have some inkling as to when this might be the case.

By structuring our interference as pharmacological, or as a manual-ised or mechanised talking therapy, we may be able to believe that we have become mere elements of the environment, which happen to the patient, rather as the weather does, and we can feel justified in leaving to the patient all responsibility for their behavioural response. This amounts to a neglect of professional responsibility. We should all work towards careful endings, but we should also pay more attention to the safety of embarking on a treatment relationship in the first place.

Attempting to keep the relationship superficial with the idea of avoiding psychodynamic pitfalls is misguided and almost certainly futile. We shall be related to as parents to some extent and so we need to be alert to the signs of being drawn into dysfunctional roles and skilled in steering a course between them.

If I were to suggest that this applies more in adult mental health, it would be a disingenuous avoidance of the responsibility to assess suitability for treatment. We argue, in child and adolescent mental health circles, that the personality is not yet developed, and we avoid using personality disorder as a diagnosis for this reason. It is a feeble argument. Personality disorder diagnoses are not very stable longitudinally through adult life either. The dynamics of personality disorder are certainly evident in many of our patients, and a degree of instability is regarded as normal in this age group. We can get into all sorts of "pickles" trying to treat some young people and we probably make them worse on occasion. I cannot wind the clock back, and might be accused of trying to do so, but I will observe that we used to argue firmly that young people in certain categories—chiefly those in abusive or unstable home environments—should not be treated until their situation was stabilised and "good enough". This was an attempt, either instinctive or well judged, to avoid fruitless and potentially damaging intervention. We have become less able to do this. Mental health legislation and local authority commissioning restrict our ability to avoid well-meant, if bumbling, attempts at treatment, but they have not been accompanied by the necessary resources and training required to make treatment of people in these situations safe.

Children are situated within an environment that to some extent buffers the effect of therapeutic interventions. This can work in either direction. When the family environment is good enough issues of transference etc. are worked through primarily within the family (that is, they are not transference at all). The relationship with the therapist and the treating system is a borrowed one and a holiday. If it helps, then all is well and good. If is inept it will be left behind (I am not talking here about manifest therapeutic abuse, which is another kettle of fish). The opposite scenario is that of the child who is in a disastrously harmful environment. In this case, although our ability to do therapy is reduced, any harm potentially caused by bumbling attempts at treatment is likely to be relatively innocuous alongside the other harms. It might be suggested that we can therefore afford to go on ignoring psychodynamic issues as far as selective matching of patient and therapy are concerned, though I would counter that this would result in a wastage of scarce resources and represent an inexcusable degree of cynicism. The correct approach in the latter scenario is clearly to do what can be done to stop the ongoing harm and establish the child in a safe and consistent home environment. Treatment can be introduced later, if that change is not sufficient.

When it comes to ending, we must consider the dynamics, because in the event, likely or otherwise, of our having achieved some therapeutic benefit for the child and family, we owe it to them all to extricate ourselves in such a way that they can retain the benefit. Furthermore, if we have become involved in complex dynamic relationships, either with our patient or their parents, we absolutely must close these appropriately. This will form part of the argument for *saying goodbye* in the last chapter.

Referral criteria

One of the greatest human fears must be the fear of being "unliveable-with". Possibly the most fundamental version of this is being able or unable to live with oneself and I suspect that we use something like social referencing to decide if that is possible. I think that it is likely that the ability to live with oneself is secondary to a plausible belief that someone else is able to tolerate being with us. The unliveable-with is outcast and will die, in our ethology as well as our phantasy. The bringing of a child to the clinic may represent an honest attempt on the part of the parents to make the child more liveable-with, but the very act enshrines the implication that they may not be. Turning him away may be done in such a way that the received message is that he is "fine" but it is just as likely to be one of untreatability and permanent unacceptability, whatever the accompanying rhetorical protestations of denial that accompany it. Being prepared—or, better, wanting—to see the child again and sit with him (even when he is not bringing what you appear to want him to bring), and finally offering him an open door for a time, may all amount to the most profound, necessary, and economical of treatments.

The chief criterion for accepting a referral in child and adolescent mental health, then, should be the level of distress and developmental disruption, rather than a set of arbitrarily defined diagnostic categories.

Writing letters

What we write in letters is an extension of what we are. It will form part of how I am experienced by my patients and those around them. Therapeutic attitude should not only be evident in the letter, but should pervade the process of its construction. If I press a button so that a machine sends you a letter, then you have not had a letter from me. If you experience it as a letter from me (which you might do, if I have signed it) it will be evident to you that there is a machine between me and you or that I am behaving like a machine. It is not the same if there is a secretary between us. Secretaries may be more expensive than machines, but they are infinitely more intelligent and responsive. The better the relationship between me and the secretary, and the more personal the secretary's involvement in the team, the more the patient and family are in a human network. They are more likely to be looked after and feel looked after, than they would be by a machine or by people behaving like machines. Furthermore, the secretary who knows me will know what I am likely to be trying to say as I stumble through a dictation. He or she will hear the tone of voice and the hesitations, and will make sense of the bits that have become tangled. This is more efficient and more human; it is more healthy. In this way the letter becomes part of the treatment.

Having sung the praises of letters, I do not believe that even the most beautifully constructed letter will "work" if the actual clinical engagement is absent, and a really good clinical engagement can usually survive a few ham-fisted letters.

Summary and treatment manifesto

- Treatment is a word that refers not only to our specific intervention, but also all the other behaviours surrounding it.
- We do not know which aspects of treatment, in this broader sense, will be of greatest therapeutic benefit, or harm, to our patient.
- All aspects therefore deserve our attention.
- Treatment should not be reflex.
- Sometimes a treatment is most helpful when held in reserve.
- Because of the power of context, all treatment should be informed by:
  o psychodynamic understanding;
  o behavioural principles;
  o systemic awareness.
- Teams and treatments, whilst preserving specific expertise, should therefore always be eclectic.

CHAPTER NINE

Saying goodbye

This chapter is different to the ones that went before. Content and process are confluent in a way that they have not been since the introductory chapters. The book ends as it talks about ending. I hope that we can explore this parallel together, though the "together" will have a rather strained aspect to it. The relationship between writer and reader is different to that between patient and clinician, though it has an asymmetry reminiscent to some degree.

The confluence of content and process in this chapter attracts my interest and I find myself reaching for joint attention, rather like a single person watching something beautiful unfold, wishing they had someone with whom to share it. I find my use of the word "you" has become more personal again. Like an unrequited lover, I have no information from you to suggest that this interest is reciprocated. Nevertheless, perhaps against all reason, I persist. The approach of separation has lent keenness to my perception of the limits to our proximity. As Emily Dickinson succinctly put it, "By a departing light / We see acuter" (1970, p. 696).

The effect, then, of the "departing light" is to give this chapter a more experimental and personal style. I shall start relatively conventionally and explain the importance of taking endings seriously. I shall then change the structure, becoming a little more assertive in my craziness;

a recapitulation of the craziness that led to my writing this book in the first place, hopefully matured and more functional by virtue of having found the words and spoken them. Clinical contact in mental health is about finding the right words with which to apprehend experience: "The Words to Say It" (Cardinal, 1983).

The most striking difference between the end of this book and the ending of a clinical episode lies in the fact that you and I did not meet at the beginning, and therefore cannot satisfactorily separate at the end. The clinical situation is not so much one of the patient bringing his finished book for the clinician to read, as bringing the agitating idea of a book to a very helpful editor and their constructing it together, neither of them remembering to commit it to print, though the editor writes some private notes to render his assistance more coherent and efficient. There is no reader, no audience. Neither clinician nor patient has, to borrow from Barenboim (2006) once more, anything "materially there to show" for the experience.

The exact point at which a relationship ends is less clear than one might imagine, as past lovers often find to their dismay. The end of the book may be its back cover and as you close it you might, so to speak, say "goodbye", but that would not necessarily signify the end of your relationship with it. If you have the inclination, you can turn back the clock and reread, much as you did the first time but, even if you don't, the relationship is likely to persist in some way, the more so for the fact that you have reached this far into it. On my part, to actually try to say "goodbye" to you would seem to me a rather trite denial of what I have just said about the limits of our relationship. We have not said "hello" so I shall not say "goodbye".

What all this reveals is that not only is there a difference between a book and a therapy, there is a difference between ending and saying *goodbye*. This section of the book is about both. It makes the point that because the physical separation can do violence to the relationship it is important to say *goodbye*. In so doing, one is propelled into the task of ending responsibly.

Why the fuss?

Why make such a big deal of the ending? Why the drum roll? In the context of a book it might be right for us to say, "This is just a book," and it would almost certainly be safe simply to stop at any point. I am only the person who wrote the words that you are reading.

Similarly, in the clinical context it might be the case that I was "only" exploring a diagnostic possibility or monitoring medication. "This isn't psychoanalysis," one might say, "so why all the fuss about ending properly?"

The answer is that one does not know for sure that the dynamics of psychotherapy have not been at play all along. In my view they will have been, at least to some extent. Indeed, society has evolved a culture of saying *goodbye*, even as one leaves the corner shop or gets off a bus. If we have evolved this acknowledgement of ending in such transient and apparently banal relationships, how much more should we do so in the clinical encounter where the agenda has been explicitly one of vulnerability and care?

As far as I can tell, the attention we give to the finish is owed to the dynamic tradition, and psychodynamic understanding is at its most evident in generic mental health work when we manage endings carefully. "Saying goodbye" is both my shorthand, and my device, for exercising clinical responsibility through that process.

Before thinking about how to end, let me list and then expand a little on why it is important to do so.

Attention should be paid to the ending because:

1. It may in itself be a significant loss. The trauma entailed should not be recklessly or sadistically imposed.
2. If there has been previous traumatic loss then efforts should be made to render the clinical ending therapeutic or restorative, providing some learning recapitulation.
3. There may be introjects, projections, and so on, that need to be shifted or restored to safe positions.
4. We pay too little attention to endings in daily life and the opportunity to live through an ending with eyes open should not be missed.
5. The ending might stand for a past ending, or it might be a rehearsal for a future one.
6. It is polite and normal to say *goodbye*, and behaviours do not evolve for no purpose.
7. Nothing is complete until completed.

These may turn out to be different ways of saying the same thing, but if this proves to be the case, my defence will be that it was such an important thing to say that it merited being said seven times.

The ending may be a significant loss

It isn't always, but one should never presume, just because the patient leaves with a cheery smile, that it isn't a significant loss. There will have been a quite stupendous degree of trust and one-sided intimacy. In case you think this a grandiose stand, consider for a second the situation in which the young person says, "This is confidential, right?" and, after our explanation of the limits of confidentiality, goes on to tell us details that would make their parents' hair curl. We are massively trusted, so let us not forget it.

The patient's intimate exposure, by the way, is met by significant intimacy on the part of the clinician, though it is intimacy of a different kind. It is not an intimacy of content, but of effort and of emotional availability. The eye contact, the pause, and the response that registers without disclosing, are carefully, if subliminally, calculated. The effort required to do this reveals an intimacy of a kind, though not one that exposes much of the therapist other than their willingness and capacity for just such a personal expenditure.

The clinical relationship has to be different to the common or garden variety, or there would be no point. The loss of it is likely, therefore, to be important. To grossly overplay its importance, on the other hand, would be another way to commit violence to it: "My doctor revealed his narcissism at the end." We are left, therefore, choosing to believe that the relationship is important, treating its ending with respect, and allowing the patient an opportunity to do so as well, avoiding the ripping away of something the importance of which they had not yet fully appreciated.

Jonathan Pedder (1988) reflected on the cruel language of "termination" and raised some interesting questions as to how absolute the ending of therapy could be. But at least the word "termination" with its brutal connotations drew attention to the possibility of it being traumatic. It therefore deserves our attention. In the epigraph to his paper, Pedder quotes Winnicott: "The mere termination of breastfeeding is not a weaning" (1988, p. 495). In the same way, the mere stopping of appointments does not constitute a therapeutic ending.

The patient's internal state and context define what is traumatic to her. We therefore should not end the relationship without some attempt to ascertain how much this could be the case, to understand, and to help the patient in her task of managing it. We should, in other words, *be with* her throughout the ending. The ending is complete when there is no more *being with* going on.

Clinical endings should be in some way therapeutic or restorative

The children and families that come to see us are more likely than most to have suffered traumatic losses. This may be because of some temperamental or physiological characteristic of the child, an illness, the structure and functioning of the family, or simply bad luck.

If there has been previous traumatic loss then this clinical ending should itself be, as a recapitulation, not merely minimally traumatic in its own right, but also therapeutic, restorative, or at the very least informative.

This is on the basis that, rather like exposure to the subject-object of a phobia, the experience of a recapitulation is likely to be either managed or unmanaged. In the context of phobia, the patient selects an exposure calculated to provoke anxiety, but dosed such that newly acquired strategies are able to contain it. If this is miscalculated, the exposure either passes as a non-event (a non-achievement), or prompts a shock and flight that sets therapy, and the patient, back.

In other words the ending can be a) an over-prepared-for non-event, b) an under-prepared-for confirmation of the post-traumatic dysfunctional schema, or c) a satisfactory therapeutic experience that moves the patient forwards, better prepared for the future. Obviously the first is preferable to the second. It is the third that one hopes for.

There may be introjects and projections that need to be shifted or restored to safe positions

Rather than attempting to handle the jargon correctly here, I shall offer three analogies that seem topical and apposite.

It is as though I were unplugging my mental and emotional circuitry from that of the patient. The risk might be similar to that encountered when removing an external hard drive from a computer. Before removal it is important to make sure that new data has been saved and that programmes have been shut down. Damage, we are led to believe, would otherwise result. For most of us this damage is of an unspecified nature—one imagines data loss or fragmentation—but one feels certain that it would be difficult or impossible to remedy. We might wish that we hadn't plugged the thing in in the first place. The timing of removal is important and activity at the interface has to be brought down to a minimum.

A simple, more human analogy might be the interrupted conversation. Why is interruption so rude? Why when we are in the middle of an argument am I so outraged when you abruptly leave?—"Don't you dare walk away from me when I am talking to you!" It may simply be that we like to have the stage, or dislike being ignored, but I suspect there is more. Each of us is leaning forwards and our interaction forms an arch. I am unbalanced if you step away and can suffer at least the indignity of a stumble; at worst, the injury of a fall.

The therapist's presence, skill, and intervention have helped the patient to rearrange himself in some transient and experimental way. He may, for a period, be responding to the therapist as he might to a parent, or he might have raised an emotional weight from where it lay on the ground in a way that would not have been possible without the therapist lending a hand. The return trajectory (which in a successful therapy is not an exact return) may not be negotiable alone, the patient left acting the role of child, or tottering under the weight of emotion.

We pay too little attention to endings in daily life. The opportunity to live through an ending with eyes open should not be missed

I shall always remember the behaviour of a good friend in New Zealand, where we had previously lived for seven years, the day we were to leave again after a two-week holiday. He was setting off for work, knowing that we would have gone by the time he returned in the evening. He drove very slowly down the grass to his gate, looking steadily at us through the open window of his car. No words were spoken, nor could any words have been spoken that could do more justice to the situation than did that protracted and unflinching gaze. At the time words would have only detracted but, for the purposes of this account, I shall suggest something along the lines of, "I am not going to let this distance develop unwitnessed. I want to be sure that the separation I shall know in the future is contiguous with, and shades into, the closeness that we have known up to now."

Tennyson's lines from "In Memoriam" (see, for example, Hayward, 1956, p. 322), written for his lost friend, are typically quoted in isolation: "'Tis better to have loved and lost/than never to have loved at all." The key, though, to the redemptive power of the stanza is in the line before: "I feel it when I sorrow most". My life is better if I have loved and lost, *provided* I am connected in some way to the love throughout and after the loss. It is to a large extent the heat of loss that forges that connection.

The ending of therapy might stand for a past ending, or it might be a rehearsal for a future one

A past ending might have been conducted with less grace and wisdom than that between my New Zealand friend and myself. I shall borrow again from the same chapter in my life. When we left New Zealand the first time, with two young children, a crowd of friends gathered in the small airport departure lounge. We talked until someone remarked that we had a plane to catch. I suppose that there were hugs and final farewells, but I remember emerging from a state of unfocused—or possibly over-focused—consciousness and realising that we had shown our boarding passes, gone through a gate, and turned a corner without my properly appreciating the fact that I was losing visual contact with my friends. Avoidance had robbed me of the experience of loss that would have confirmed the reality of the attachment. I had not, at that stage, had the benefit of the parting described above. I have set them out here in reverse chronological order, describing the therapy before the trauma. I am a different person now, and hope always to have the courage to turn away consciously when I have to.

The point is that attention should be paid to loss as it happens in order to affirm and forge the connection. Emily Dickinson wrote, "Pain—has an Element of Blank," going on to tell us that "it cannot recollect" (1970, p. 323). Perhaps Dickinson's pain cannot recollect for the same reason that traumatic loss cannot be assimilated, namely that the subject is not sufficiently there to lay down or retrieve memories. Traumatic loss, like any traumatic experience, causes problems because the necessary avoidance of the immediate devastation or damage prevents us from paying attention to the loss at the crucial moment. We are crouching with eyes tight shut, or may have vacated our selves entirely. Some reparation can occur later when a similar or parallel loss is handled more consciously and with greater wisdom, and this can also act as a rehearsal for future parting.

I am sure it has been said somewhere that life is spent recovering from the trauma of entering it and preparing for the trauma of leaving. This might be too cynical and bitter. On the other hand, to say that these two traumas are the pillars that hold up the temple arch would be a little too trite for me. I suggest that life amounts to a cycle with three phases, repeated in a fractal pattern: arrival, existence, and departure; connection (or engagement), *being with*, separation. The terms we use will depend on our perspective and style but the shape is always the same.

It is polite and normal to say goodbye, and behaviours do not evolve without purpose

Just because this is a special, or professional, relationship, one should not remove the normal social niceties. Despite it being normal and polite to say goodbye, we generally don't do it very well. In fact, in our daily lives we are notoriously bad at it. I have been at a number of two-day courses in various therapeutic activities (where one might expect participants to know better) and have often been struck by the ritualistic exchange of names and addresses that usually takes place as they draw to a close. I say ritualistic because these exchanges are largely symbolic and stereotyped, and serve a purpose other than the apparent one of exchanging the information that would allow future communication. I do not believe that, in the most part, these people contact each other afterwards. Some will, but they were there to make friends rather than do the work. Eventually the lists of names and email address are jettisoned. The practice is to enable them to sidestep, or overlook, the fact of ending. In a more prosaic example, people who have enjoyed each other's company but are almost certainly never to see one another again, commonly part with a cheerful, "See you!" It seems that we dance our way through transitions.

Behaviours, though, tend not to evolve without a purpose. In Darwinian terms they persist and propagate because they have some survival value. This should not be enough for us to adopt them uncritically. Dawkins (1976) pointed out that it may be the genes that are surviving and propagating, rather than the individuals that carry them. Not all successful gene mutations—characteristics, behaviours—will be in the individual's interests. If "cheerio" evolved it may be because it speeds things up, leaves the past behind, and attracts another mate. The "cheerio" moves on and multiplies, never serving the vector very well.

I suggest that we "walk the line" once more; that we say *goodbye* because it is normal and polite to do so, even employing some societal norms, but that we think about what we are doing as we do so. Rituals work better if someone present knows what they are for.

Considering what this evolved ritual might mean, brings me to the importance of acknowledgement by one of the other. A crucial aspect of therapeutic work with children is the forming of a respectful relationship with them: discussing, offering genuine choices, and relating to them as valid, motivated humans with a right to, and the potential for, a life of their own, rather than simply existing as a product and part of the lives of others. To acknowledge the end of a relationship is to confirm that it existed and was real. If I take it seriously, then it was real for me. This child has left a footprint on a foreign shore.

That the relationship was real for me is particularly important for the child, but, interestingly, even more important than *my* goodbye to him is *his to me*. Parents frequently acknowledge this without knowing why, when they leave a favoured holiday spot, for example. "Bye-bye beach!" is chanted without any expectation that the beach will reply. I cannot imagine an untroubled child waiting for a reply, or being upset if there wasn't one. The child has said goodbye to a place that has been important. That was necessary and sufficient.

Of course, when I refer to the importance of the child or the patient "saying goodbye" I am not referring to the use of those words, but the act. The words, like the grudgingly mumbled "sorry", do not mean what they say if they are spoken under instruction. What will matter more is the eye contact or some other gesture. A couple of days before drafting this paragraph a mother and daughter (I shall call her Lucy) left my room after a first appointment which had given them each some positive expectation. The mother and I said goodbye in a friendly and proper way that encouraged me to believe that there was engagement and then the mother told her daughter to say goodbye. This was fine. Lucy spoke a faint "goodbye". All of this meant that her mother knew the social importance and Lucy was well behaved. What I took to be more significant was the brief eye contact as she did so. The tone of my reply conveyed, I hope, an understanding that Lucy had emitted one "goodbye" for her mother and another for me.

So my goodbye to the child is polite, it signifies the existence of the child and the reality of our relationship, now coming to an end, and it is also a prompt for the child to say goodbye to me. In so doing he fulfils his half of a contract, leaves a mark on the world, forges a connection with loss, and takes with him something that is his own.

Nothing is complete until completed

The proof of the pudding is in the eating, and the proof of a connection is the loss experienced when it is ended. An unfinished task may be thought to live forever, but in a way it has not even been born. The ending of something is the final act of bringing it fully into existence. This is what it means to live moment by moment. Each thing comes fully into existence at the moment at which it ends. If it were not ended, it would still be amenable to change and so would be indistinct, corruptible, and undefined. Of course, it may not be practical to live all of one's life like that. That is one of the intrusions of reality. We cannot all be Buddhist mendicants. But there are some things best left done.

If the patient invests the clinician with knowledge of his insides—of *dia-gnosis*—then he really needs to know whether it is an ongoing relationship or not. It is fine to have a relationship with your GP that lasts a lifetime—in fact I think it is what people want and possibly need—dipping in and out, feeling held and understood, but the nature of a specialist service is that it starts and then it finishes. We know when the builders have gone because they take their tools away. It is only then that we can look around and take stock, hopefully with some relief and satisfaction, before resuming our lives. Moving on without taking stock would be risky. Taking stock when there is still someone traipsing in and out, carrying stuff, would be pointless. So ending properly is required so that the event and its contents can be sealed and ratified, enabling us to move forwards.

There is a contract between one and another when they meet. It is to follow the trajectory described above: meet, act, leave. Even in marriage the contract includes a promise to depart. In Anthony Minghella's 1990 film, *Truly, Madly, Deeply*, the dead Jamie breaks this aspect of the contract and his persistent presence, initially welcomed by a still-grieving Nina, increasingly interferes. His departure, allowed by her, is necessary for her to move on.

If someone offers to tell you a story, and then stops before the end, or if the novel you are reading or the film you are watching peters out in an unsatisfactory way, you feel cheated. The contract is one you would not have entered into if it did not include a proper ending.

A hardback book needs both covers. The front attracts us to it, but without the back cover it falls apart. Of the two—arrival and departure—it is the latter that needs to be, and can be, in clearer focus.

At the beginning we have only our fantasy to go on, and a notion of infinite time in which to explore what it is that we have entered into. At the end we have more information, but a deadline after which the opportunity ceases. We are, therefore, better resourced for clear vision as well as in greater need of it.

A final letter

As letter writing has been part of the process and is such a concrete form of communication, the last letter deserves some attention. Some therapies—to my knowledge most notably CAT (cognitive analytic therapy) (Ryle & Kerr, 2002)—make letter writing an important part of the therapy itself, but I shall not delve into this here. I have argued that all letters should be more therapeutic than otherwise and I think that this applies most of all to a last letter.

In thinking about the importance of letter writing, I shall bear in mind the strong likelihood that most letters will make little impression on my young patient. I don't believe for a moment that this means that the writing can be taken lightly. The letter can stand for a part of the clinician that the patient can take and keep. As it has come out of the clinician's head it can simultaneously imply that the clinician has kept something of the patient in them. It may be thrown in the bin or kept in a file by the parent, but it has the potential to signify many things. It has travelled in vans, on conveyer belts, and in mailbags, and has reached the house. It has survived.

It is a concrete remnant from an encounter that might have otherwise been considered a dream and suggests that things from this kind of dream, at least, can be brought into actuality. It is reminiscent of that device in films and stories in which the protagonist awakes from a dream and finds that something—a feather or other small object—from the dream has appeared in the room. The dream reality, whilst it can be distanced, cannot be utterly discounted.

The discharge or goodbye letter is not a transitional object. Parents sometimes make the mistake of believing that they can choose, create, or provide a transitional object for their child but the child has to discover/create this themselves. The letter cannot take on this degree of power and flexibility. It is more like a cloakroom ticket. My older brother once took a group of family members punting. I was young at the time and worried that the punt might overturn. He gave me his jacket to hold as a guarantee that this would not happen. There was no logic to this at all—we were all in the same boat—but I was completely calmed by this stroke of genius on his part. I think that my holding his jacket gave me a firm link to the confidence that I lacked but existed in him.

It may be unlikely that the letter will serve any magical function of this kind—but it has that potential. It will not be framed and hung on the wall. It is much more likely to be lost. But it has the capacity to connect my patient with the confidence in relation to her that I have in me and that she may not have in herself.

There is a meaning in the opposite direction. This formal, distanced manifestation of myself suggests that I have written similar letters to others. Perhaps many others. This is a more subtle learning than would be the sight of me absorbed in pushing my child on a swing, or standing proudly at a degree ceremony. These would be more brutal because I would not only be available to another, but would be altogether lost to the patient. I would have ceased to be who and what I had been to them previously. No longer a doctor. The doctor is dead or sadistic. In the more gentle letdown, the doctor is still a doctor, but has stepped back.

The social parting gift sets up a contradiction. At the same moment as the contact is lost, something of the lost object is more incontrovertibly possessed than ever before. It is an inverse reflection of what happens when the infant encounters the mother as another being: she is obtained and simultaneously lost because her otherness becomes apparent at the moment that she comes into focus. There is something "take it or leave it" about a relationship that is ongoing. The other need never be held because it can always be accessed. Gifts, like concrete memories, begin to belong exactly when the opportunity to constantly refresh the external connection is lost.

The letter is from me and the words must be mine. They must offer a plausible representation of me. If I have managed to understand the patient then the letter should also represent him in some way, as well as doing justice to the therapeutic work.

I try to think of the letter, even if addressed to others, as a communication with my patient. The wording must allude to what has happened to a sufficient extent, without betraying confidences. It is also a communication to the parents, usually the referring GP, and sometimes other professionals. It needs to be grammatical and professional.

> Here is a fairly simple discharge letter to a GP:
>
> Dear Dr. …,
>
> re Sasha so-and-so …
>
> Following my letter to you of 7 April I saw Sasha on a further four occasions. He managed to talk very frankly about some of the difficulties he has been experiencing and has, I think, discovered a way to set these alongside his perfectly reasonable aspirations. He has learned and practised a number of psychological techniques, including mindfulness, and has become better at knowing when they may be most useful. It will be helpful to him to continue to practise them on a regular basis.
> We decided that he does not need to come to CAMHS any more and I have discharged him from my clinic. If you want to discuss this more please feel free to get in touch with me. Sasha and his parents know that they can come to you if they need to and, although I doubt it will come to this, I would be happy to see him again if re-referral were to become necessary between now and his eighteenth birthday.
> It has been a pleasure working with Sasha and I wish him all the best for the future.
> With best wishes, etc.

I have chosen a fairly banal example after my extravagant claims for the symbolic importance, partly to bring us back down to earth, but it is worth looking at some of the wording in more detail:

1. He "managed" to talk. In other words it was not easy for him. There may be some self-promotion on my part, but there is also a nod to Sasha for his own achievement, and the fact of his uphill struggle. This might give his parents pause for thought, but it will also let them off the very uncomfortable hook that many parents fashion for themselves out of the fact that adolescents very often don't talk easily to their parents.
2. The phrase "some of the difficulties he has been experiencing" may be a reference to difficulties his parents cause him or problems in personal relationships. Sasha, his parents, and the GP may each think that they know what this refers to. (If there was a concern about his safety, this will have been dealt with in much more explicit terms, either therapeutically or in collaboration with other agencies.)

3. My explicit distancing from the know-all position is conveyed by the "some" and the "I think". This may allow Sasha to find useful take-home messages from the treatment episode, even if he doesn't agree with everything I have said.

4. The fact that he wants to do something with his life is itself an achievement. The problem is that his parents either don't approve or they don't think him capable. The phrase, "perfectly reasonable" allows his aspirations to be fleetingly imagined as "perfect" whereas they are, in my view, merely "reasonable". To call them simply "reasonable" without the "perfectly" would, however, have been rather mean-spirited. At the same time "perfectly reasonable" conveys a degree of impatience with his parents' doubts, which were undermining his self-esteem.

5. The bit about the techniques is partly to let the parents and the GP know that something "real" has been done. And indeed so it has. These are useful techniques that had to be learned and need to be practised. This was the explicit work. At least as important, though, are the covert messages about Sasha's achievement in the face of difficulty, and his viability—his reality as a person—underlined by the fact that we decided the ending together.

6. I said that I enjoyed working with him because I did. Working with young patients is the best thing about my job.

I don't know how much of this reaches its destination. I don't really mind if it doesn't. Everyone will know that he is discharged and can be re-referred, but the connections and meanings are available. The point is that they are therapeutic meanings and connections, rather than casual or dismissive ones.

The final straight

Having made the case for taking ending seriously—for *saying goodbye*—it remains only to do so. We have explored *being with* and then moved through engagement, assessment, and treatment. There were premonitions of ending from the outset, but now, as we gear down, the engine sounds change.

Dividing ending up into sections does not work very well because the sections merge. Everything, from contemplating ending, through the farewells and the last door closing, even to later reflections, is part of the process.

For this reason, instead of headings I have numbered the remaining paragraphs in order, descending towards the end of the chapter and of the book proper. The last paragraph will be "paragraph zero". In this way you will have an idea of where you are and the last paragraph should not come as a surprise.

Ending crops up in different forms and guises throughout the duration of a clinical relationship. It is a little like the writing through a stick of rock. Wherever you break it, it is there. The rest of this chapter is broken into pieces. Each of them has "goodbye" printed through it. You can read them in any order, provided that you read paragraph zero at the end—and dispose of the wrapper responsibly.

24. The end of treatment is a sort of death. All relationships carry potential and any categorical separation is the termination of that potential. Therapeutic ending is a death that can be approached knowing the time and the circumstances, with honest acknowledgement. The idea of concomitant birth is a reasonable one with some substance, but it is important that it not be used like a sugar dummy to silence and distract from the fact of ending.

23. In attempting to discern a difference between preparing for ending and ending we might do worse than think about where the process takes place. Preparation for ending should be happening in the clinician's mind pretty much all the time, but when preparation becomes overt in the exchanges between clinician and patient, I would consider this to be the ending actually in process.

22. To make the ending overt at the outset would be unhelpful in the same way that it is unhelpful to lovers, upon their falling in love, to deflate the process with a prediction of betrayal or disenchantment. It would be cruel to the child in them. On the other hand it could be cruel to encourage a fantasy that there will be no ending. A healthy toddler is likely to be distrustful of a stranger greeting them, even if welcomed by his parent. After an hour or so, and the coffee drunk, when the stranger gets up to leave she may notice that the child

is chatting to her. She has become more acceptable by virtue of the fact that she is going. But all of this is properly located out of mind. I cannot recall a child, at the start of the treatment episode, expressing anxiety about either an endless relationship, or one that will end too soon. Their concern is usually more about whether or not they want to be there at all. Provided the therapeutic attitude is there, the ending can be called to mind or made to disappear according to need.

21. I often think of the necessary lie that a parent tells a child (indeed, we tell each other all the time) on parting: "I will be back soon." The autistic truth would be that I hope or intend to be back soon, but what will actually transpire is in the lap of the gods. This would terrify and incapacitate the child. In the same, way we assume the follow-up appointment will occur and I shall conduct it and we gloss over the fact of an ending at some point in such a way that the child can decommission his abandonment alarm system and turn his attention to the work. At some point, though, it is important to acknowledge that this time will come to an end and, if the patient raises it, the question of ending should be explored at that point, rather than skirted or deferred.

20. If waiting amounts, like so much else of therapeutic attitude, to sitting on a fence, then we need to practise sitting on the fence for long periods of time without, as an adult patient once said to me, "someone shoving a post up your arse". We must not become rigid or fixed. Sitting on the fence requires balance and carries the risk of falling. In the transition between not-even-thinking-about-ending and now-we-are-ending, we need to be able to shift our balance with such grace and style that we can un-fall if we need to, if the moment was wrong. In Tai Chi we are taught to walk in such a way that weight is transferred from one foot to the other without at any point being committed to the transfer. It must be possible to move backwards at any point, never "falling" from one foot to the next. This fence-sitting is similar. I might put my "ending" foot down, but if it is not right I can move my weight back off it and be exactly as I was before.

19. The experience, perception, and perhaps even the reality, of time are different for children by virtue of the pace and scale of the

development that they are undergoing. I shall leave it to those who practise with adults to argue whether or not the same can be true for adults. I suspect the answer will depend on the degree of regression in the patient.

Pip had had a number of monthly sessions with her mother until she felt ready to have them independently. By then she was seventeen. Fairly soon we began to perceive an ending, initially as a possibility and then as something that was certainly going to happen. When, in discussing possible resources available after discharge, I made it clear that she would not be coming back to my clinic because it was a child and adolescent service, she looked around her, as though for the first time, and said, "God, I'm such an idiot!" In the room there was a doll's house and a plastic garage with cars. The lower bookshelves held a couple of rows of books ranging from chunky ones with flaps instead of words, to *Where's Wally* and football manuals. There was a low table with two tiny chairs and a tub of coloured pencils. We brought this realisation into the next couple of sessions and reflected on how she had effectively grown up here. It was essential for her to appreciate this so that she could know what it was that she was leaving behind. And it illustrated for me the timelessness and the subjectivity of the experience for my patients. To set a limit at the outset of that work would have rendered it useless.

---

18. One can argue that there is a rehearsal of ending as each appointment or session closes. My view is that this is only a rehearsal once the real ending has been acknowledged. This is the case from the outset if one is practising a therapy limited by either time or number of sessions. From that point of acknowledgement onwards, the end of each appointment takes on a special significance that can be recognised or denied, but which is there. Before that stage it may be acceptable for appointments to rush to a close, end with a nod, or falter and peter out in a *laissez-faire* way, the behaviour interpreted at the next appointment, or not, depending on the treatment modality. The goodbye is replaced, on all these pre-ending occasions, with agreed arrangements for the next appointment.

17. The end may be planned to a specific date, or could be through an explicit process of weaning. The approach decided on will be the product of agreement between clinician and patient and will depend on the nature of the work. Future dates may be notional or "hover", to be settled upon later. A variation on this, that requires more "holding in mind" by the clinician, is an understanding that

at some point in the future, perhaps after a year, a letter will be written, offering an appointment. This requires a robust system of caseload management and not too many distractions. I think it is better, though, to allow a "long stop offer" to drift past its intended limit, than to fire off a mechanistic appointment date.

16. I do not practise the kinds of therapies, necessary within a comprehensive service, that set an ending at the outset. In my current clinical role to do so would have a degree of arbitrariness to it and might betray a lack of *being with* in that it would suggest that I already knew best before I had started to listen. The closest I come to this, generally speaking, is to agree a number of appointments followed by review, making a point of not ending the therapy without sufficient approach for it to be prepared for and worked on if necessary. Even if an ending is planned, it may not take place *as* planned.

15. These reflections and the practice that has evolved amount to a deliberate means by which my patient can feel "held" by my continued existence as long as that is required. What I am attempting to demonstrate is an attentive flexibility, knowledge of the terrain, and willingness to "play" with ideas of confidence, autonomy, and loss. To counteract the smorgasbord impression, here is what I do *not* do: I do not make a unilateral decision to discharge someone without an attempt to negotiate and find out something about its meaning to them. I am doing what I can to avoid both rejection and negligence in the process of ending.

14. At what stage can I relax? Once again, I appear to be attempting to occupy an impossible space. I am attempting to *be with* my patient right up to that point when we are no longer with one another, and yet not to have an abrupt transition. It is an indefinable moment, like the end of a sound or the point where we fall asleep. I can remember trying as a child to identify the actual point at which I fell asleep. Inevitably I failed. The closest I came was to identify a sort of mental letting go that I took to be a signal that I would soon be asleep. I don't recall much consciousness after that, so perhaps that was it. So what is happening may be a similar mental letting go, and the moment of recognising it is the moment at which it "happens".

13. What matters is the psychological, as opposed to the physical, separation and this, too, contributes to the impossibility of identifying the exact time of the end. There is a physical separation at the end of each appointment, but the doctor and patient have not ended their therapeutic relationship. The child's understanding that physical removal does not necessarily mean an end to the relationship has Piagetian and other developmental significance. Much of development seems to be to do with, first, perception and acknowledgement of otherness, followed by acquiring an ability to manipulate the experience: calling things up through imagination or desire, coping with delay, and so on. A child, after a certain stage, knows that an object can (and usually does) continue to exist even though it has ceased to be visible. He can access it for himself if he can find the key to its location, and has the necessary strength and/or permission. Ideally the child is not introduced to the unequivocal disappearing act that is death until these preliminary versions have been well mastered.

12. Up to the point of separation the clinician's thoughts are plausibly accessible to the patient. From that point on, the latter has only memories of those of the clinician's thoughts that were communicated, some physical record, and the ability to imagine what new thoughts might have arisen in the fresh circumstance. Up until that time there was the opportunity for the patient to update the clinician, apprising her of developments. But from then on, whilst the child can imagine that the clinician still has a version of him in her mind, it is inescapable that it is, if it exists, no longer contemporary or accurate. The imagined clinician can no longer be omnipotent.

11. Where there has not been an explicit last session, the closing of the file is the explicit ending. "Closing the file" is language that comes from the pre-digital era. The fact that computers persist with language and a graphic user interface recalling concrete objects is significant. It may just be my age and the fact that I have worked through the digital revolution, but it feels to me as though I am less likely to drop a patient if he has a solid avatar, as opposed to some representation in the digital cloud. Closing the file, digital or otherwise, is a considered clinical action the timing of which has, increasingly, to "fly beneath the radar" as non-clinical pressures demand time-limited interventions with documented discharge

within a fixed time of treatment onset, or whenever there is no "active clinical involvement". This *bureaucratic* attitude implies that psychodynamic life does not take place between appointments, or in the imaginations of patients and family. It ignores the toxicity of anxiety and the protective effect of being "held in mind". Keeping the file open makes it possible for me to "forget" a patient at my end, whilst she remains unforgotten by me at hers. Like stop-start technology in a car, this dormant remembering that can be fired up instantly if needed is economical of fuel and is responsive and safe.

10. I do end my work with patients around their eighteenth birthday, if not long before. The faculties of the Royal College of Psychiatrists and the General Medical Council might argue with my embarking on work with a patient when she is already eighteen, but my argument for continuing, once begun, has sound professional foundations and is stronger the more embedded in the work we are. It seems clear that developmental concerns and the context of the patient should play a greater role in determining to what extent specific child and adolescent expertise is appropriate, than should chronological age. The presence of a demarcation with legal significance is helpful, however. It provides me with limits. There is something in the idea that child and adolescent mental health professionals have something of the adolescent about us in our relationships with boundaries. I do like to push, but I need something to push against. An eighteen-year-old may require further psychiatric or psychological work. If it is the latter I usually tell him that it is better if he does not start another therapeutic relationship straight away if possible, because this can amount to an avoidance of the *goodbye* as well as a way of messing up the next treatment. In the language of romance, it is generally not a good idea to go into therapy "on the rebound".

9. There will be a closing letter. It may simply inform the referrer of discharge, but the content may summarise what has taken place. This is a delicate and important process and the use of language is crucial. I am still not an authority on the experience of my patient so it is not for me to say what has happened to them. It is an opportunity for me to allude to the otherness of the patient and the respect I have

for that. The letter is what I believe and is allowed to be so, but there should be no surprises for the patient. As well as providing a narrative, some revision, and an object that can be used in a symbolic way if necessary, I am also letting the patient know how it was for me, in some small but significant way. This is part of underlining our changed roles and separation, but it is also another way to make what happened real. If I say that I have enjoyed working with the young person and his family, it will be because I did. If it was difficult, I may say so. If I suspect that it was dissatisfying for him, I may say that too, though I would add a hope that he had found something of use in it—because he may yet do so, even after the event. Being let go of may have been the most important bit of the encounter for him, and it may be the letter that allows this.

Dear Publisher,

Thank you for putting me in touch with this reader.

I am writing to you before we reach the end of the book, copying in the reader, in the hope that it may amuse, but also allow them an opportunity to read a letter written by me, albeit in rather stretched circumstances.

To be honest, I do not know what they made of the chapters that we negotiated together. Without any feedback from them, and because of the inflexibility of the medium, I was unable to adjust my language or elaborate on any aspects that they either did not understand or did not agree with. At least they could take the work at their own pace to some extent and I have little doubt that they will have done this in most cases.

I did what you asked of me in relation to the references. I think that you are aware of my concern that this approach might be a little formal and might give the impression that the work aspired to more academic pretensions than was actually the case. I was particularly worried that this treatment ran counter to the crucial point that I hoped to get across in relation to the increasing authority of a spurious objectivity. However, I can only trust that they will understand the constraints I was under and that the irony will not be lost on them.

I have enjoyed their imagined company whilst writing and am genuinely delighted that they have remained engaged thus far. Hopefully they will have recognised enough in what I say for the whole to have been provocative in some constructive way.

Thank you, again, for the opportunity.

Yours, etc.

8. I have had the occasional letter of thanks from parents and children. I know, on the other hand, that not everyone is happy. The service now showers discharged patients with problem-saturated questionnaires. It calls to mind a young tree, once grown, cut down simply to get a good look at the growth rings, though that is probably too drastic an image. It certainly seems to be a perverse and untimely stage at which to introduce my own neurotic needs. I suspect that the information obtained is not particularly valid, and that the cost outweighs the benefit, at least from a therapeutic perspective. I would be interested to know how many of my patients were in school, further education, employment, and relationships—how many had hobbies and friends—if someone could non-intrusively gather that information on my behalf. We know that the patient is on a developmental trajectory and that his abilities and challenges will change as well as his circumstances. There should be no belief that "everything will be OK", but there could be a sense that he and his family have, or can find, the resources needed to manage most of what is thrown at them. In a sense we are all OK. It is the loss of the feeling of adequacy that is threatening. If that is the case, then if a sense of adequacy is established by discharge, then the timing is right and the treatment a success.

7. There are some patients who are, at least for a time, un-dischargeable. They are not necessarily those with the most alarming symptoms, or an Axis I disorder (APA, 1994), or those on medication (though that can be a reason for retaining a medical relationship, for example, in ADHD). It is likely to be those whose parental system cannot contain and manage the necessary anxieties. Sometimes even then they can be discharged. I have discharged adolescent patients with a mutual acknowledgement that they will have to continue to shoulder a greater proportion of the burden of containment than they should, because their parents for whatever reason are not up to the task. This is not to blame the parents. Everyone knows that child-rearing is a big "ask" and that, apart from living itself, it is about the only task one takes on without fully informed consent, but cannot then lay down. We all do what we can.

6. The ending, when confronted, might be expected to bring with it some sadness, but I have not particularly noticed this, and when

I have suggested it there has not been any significant deepening of the rapport. In other words, as Malan tells us, it was probably not a relevant or accurate interpretation. What I have encountered more often is anger. This is not usually overtly directed towards me. The patient typically defends me from her own anger, ostensibly directing it towards caregivers or professionals in general, or people "not being there for me", etc. I do not force the transference interpretation but I "notice" that she is experiencing these feelings at the same time as the ending is approaching, heralding the time when I will actually no longer "be there" for her, and I will tentatively link it with a past abandonment or loss.

5. I have to be as ready to be of no importance to my patient as I have to be ready for the opposite. What I must do is provide sufficient opportunity for him to take the relationship and its ending seriously, but to be able to let him walk off without a backward glance if that is what he needs to do. All this emphasis on ending is not to gratify my own narcissistic needs or assuage my insecurity. Like the parent at the school gates, I console myself that it is healthy for the child to march off, mingling with the crowd or even in solitude, without a backward glance. And, like those people who wave at trains, I take some consolation from the fact that, if there are any, the "up you signs come three miles further down the line" (McGough, 1982, p. 12).

4. The end is when what's "mine" becomes mine again, and the patient internalises from therapy whatever has been discovered or created and may be of future use. The patient takes away a number of things if the clinical contact and its ending have been successful. We know that the prognosis for adolescents is improved if they have encountered certain supportive and functional others with whom they have been able to form healthy relationships. Provided the ending is non-traumatic, this memory of functional attachment itself may be enough to help the young person in the future. Also there may have been factual and schematic learning with the development of a wider and healthier repertoire of ways of being. I think that one of the most important internalised goods that may be retained by the patient is an understanding that there need be no panicked rush from where we are; that we therefore

may find the time we thought we did not have: less need to change, an opportunity to understand, and a sense of having the right and the ability to make choices, even if not yet or in every instance, at least sometime and somewhere.

3. I have spoken from time to time about autonomy. This is something that babies lack and that people are generally considered to acquire. Although I am reluctant to talk about human rights, because they are matters of opinion and are either granted by the powerful or assumed by all in times of luxury, but I am inclined to the view that if there is to be any sense in the notion of being born at all, there must be some right to a degree of autonomy. Leaving aside the thankfully rare degenerative conditions, at the end of a clinical encounter with CAMHS, I do believe that a child or adolescent should have acquired some greater autonomy. No one is completely autonomous, of course, and what is probably sought is more like a functional, flexible, and instrumental dependence. Hopefully we can develop at least some autonomy from neurotic, fear-governed drives, both our own and those of others. The autonomy that the patient and his family unequivocally need for discharge, and for saying goodbye, is the autonomy that enables them to operate without the assistance of the clinician.

2. The parents' anxieties for their child do not cease when she turns eighteen, but getting her safely to that point through trials for all concerned is a special achievement. "Whatever else we have done," the parents can say, "and whatever is to come, we have at least done this one thing." They have delivered her, carried her further, and delivered her a second time at the landmark of legal majority.

Phil, already encountered in Chapter Eight, had last seen me a year and a half previously, at which time he had been almost free of tics. He surprised me by turning eighteen without my having arranged a review. I telephoned and his mother said he was still off medication and had a part-time job. His tics had come back but he wasn't bothered by them. Nevertheless, she thought he would like to see me one more time before I closed the file. They arrived a few weeks later: a very proud mother and a gentle giant, mild, friendly, smiling, and with constant tics of face and neck which, whilst obvious, didn't interrupt his communication or confidence in any way. He had an interview for a full-time job the next day. We discussed his approach to that, and rehearsed relaxation and mindfulness exercises during which his tics subsided and his mother nearly fell asleep. He confirmed that he still didn't want medication but that he knew he could go to his GP if he changed his mind. I told him what I would say in my letter to his GP and, as we shook hands, his mother said, "It's almost sad isn't it? Eleven years old I think he was." I said, "Even I was young back then!" The young man grinned and they went down the narrow stairs for the last time.

I think Phil's mother's request for this appointment was an acknowledgement that I had shared in some way in the achievement of majority. I did not feel that we had invited one another to a degree ceremony. I felt that, in requesting the clinic appointment, they had invited me to a mini birthday party. They identified this moment as an opportunity for a ritual of shared pleasure. Our respective roles were established by the casual playing of "doctor and patient", but there was no urgency in this, or purpose other than to structure the time around the important matter of saying goodbye.

1. The doctor is something of an archetype and, as such, may be something that a person has in his life throughout, without necessarily being conscious of it or directly affected by it, like death or gender. If that is the case, then I simply inhabit the role for the duration of this clinical contact (a little like for the duration of this book). Perhaps this is why I greet patients for the first time as though they are familiar to me. When a child attends for the first clinic appointment he very likely has no idea what a child and adolescent psychiatrist is or will be like (often parents will have simply told him that they are going to see the doctor). By the end of that appointment I shall have performed one function, at least, which is to put a face and a manner to the role. Future child and adolescent psychiatrists, psychiatrists, doctors, and clinicians may be a bit like me, and a bit different. The point being that, upon saying goodbye, the patient takes with him, as well as memories and suchlike, an internal doctor who may be a bit like me, but will be *his* version of doctor. This doctor may be of assistance by being called to mind consciously or unconsciously, but also by providing a way marker to the existence of further similar flesh and blood skilled companionship in the future: a professional who can provide an answering call to that of

her remembered counterpart, should further clinical contact be necessary.

0. A paragraph back I wrote "the duration of this book". Did that slip by unnoticed? As the end of the book approaches I shall suggest that we are threatened by another, more sinister, *goodbye* on the horizon. I have attempted to describe something precious. Not only have I attempted to describe it, I am still trying to deliver it in practice. That task is unquestionably becoming harder to perform. I am afraid that it may be becoming impossible. Whilst each patient I see may still be able to be brought to a satisfactory parting from me and ending of his or her treatment episode, and whilst this book may be safely closed, and the relationship between its author and its reader brought satisfactorily to a point where it exists only in each party's imagination or memory, I do *not* believe that therapeutic attitude can safely be put down. I am hoping that this book may not only facilitate genuinely therapeutic treatments, but also go some way towards preventing the loss, from public and professional life, of non-material values, reflective and open-minded engagement, and appreciation of the diversity of individual development. There was, it turns out, a messianic grandiosity to this project, after all.

EPILOGUE

Placing this after the ending may seem like providing an unscheduled appointment after a clinical closure. It would not have fitted well into the arc of the book, and yet needs to be addressed to some extent. What follows is intended to go some way towards addressing two matters that can be expected to arise from what went before.

One is the question of how to prevent the loss of professionalism that I believe to be currently underway. The other is the predictable, utilitarian, and materialistic argument that my proposal is impracticable for economic reasons.

Leaving aside the question of whether enough money is being spent on mental health services, I believe that *being with* could, in the long run, result in savings whilst maintaining clinical standards and professionalism.

An important aspect of maintaining and handing on professional values and expertise is for the trainee and the trainer to *be with* one another over time. The virtues (Radden & Sadler, 2010) of professionalism are demonstrated, acquired, and encouraged, more than taught and learned. This is apprenticeship. It requires co-location and co-working over a period of time. By a similar process, stable teams become stronger and greater than the sum of their parts.

The factual information required for professional practice can be transferred by seminars, written word, demonstrations, lectures, and so on. For effective transfer of necessary values, attitude, and the *ghost in the machine* something more like the *being with* of the apprenticeship model is needed. What happens between the lines is difficult to put into words, but is absorbed, partly subliminally and possibly all the better for it. The resistance of experienced professionals to innovations is generally poorly articulated, often falling back on emotional language, and this can earn the professions a reputation for protectionism, obstruction, or senile inertia. I suspect that much of this reluctance to adopt rapid change is to do with an intuitive understanding that it disrupts these absorbed and inherited between-the-lines ways of doing things.

A professional is likely to nurture her own and others' professionalism if she is respected for her practice. This respect will come from each of the following groups: her patients, colleagues, other professional groups, her employer, friends and family, and the public at large. She should be able to tolerate temporary loss of respect from one or two sources, provided the others continue. This flow of respect will accumulate and be translated into self-respect. This must be maintained at a healthy level—neither too high nor too low. The inarticulate component of the learning and the requirement for self-respect together constitute a weakness.

The organisation that employs the professional "knows" that quantity will be purchased at the expense of quality. This trade-off is inevitable, but it will very rarely be openly acknowledged. Indeed, organisations are likely to describe the service they provide as "excellent" with increasing desperation as the demands increase and resources are overwhelmed. There will be, inherent in this arrangement, a gap between the rhetoric and the reality (Ballatt & Campling, 2011). Denial of this introduces dishonesty that therefore becomes endemic in the system. The professional is likely to be placed under pressure to reconcile the irreconcilable. He will do his best, but he will feel and inhabit this conflict more than anyone else, because he is the one in personal and compassionate contact with the patient. He is placed in an impossible situation by the demands of his employment contract to adopt this systemic denial, meet the expectations of clinical demand, uphold the good name of his employer, and declare the care that is delivered to be "excellent". Even if this were possible, it would be inconsistent with the maintenance of probity.

High-level denial of the irreconcilable conflict between quality and volume, and the Batesonian double bind that it places around professionals and their probity, is likely to become the single biggest threat to professionalism. If volume is sacrificed to quality, the professional earns the disrespect of his employer and, to some extent, colleagues and team. If, on the other hand, quality is sacrificed to volume, he loses the respect of his patients and himself, and risks a major mishap, a malpractice suit, and erasure.

The attitude of *being with* is one that aligns squarely with the quality agenda. Adopted and promoted at organisational and national levels, respectively, it would counteract this destructive process. I shall explain the ways in which I believe it could also address the problem of volume. Some of what I claim would theoretically be testable, though very long-term follow-up is problematic and, as I am advocating something that is primarily non-utilitarian and process-oriented, the assessment of outcomes would be, by definition, beside the point.

First, moralised and re-moralised professionals are more efficient and effective than their demoralised counterparts.

Second, effort expended in the right way early on is repaid over the years in a way that misplaced effort is not. A well-parented child is likely to parent well, and a well-treated person will treat others well. Furthermore, I think that it need not require a huge intensity of treatment to respond sensitively to the needs of the young person along the lines that I have suggested. In fact, I think that a small nudge delivered at the right time is likely to be more effective than a dozen hard shoves delivered inopportunely.

Third, because compassion assists at some level, even when material improvement is not attainable, a return to compassionate, individualised, values-based care that addresses the non-material needs (which may or may not be of particular relevance in mental health care) instead of simply chasing mass-defined, material, and measurable outcomes, is likely to be both more effective and more efficient than non-compassionate care.

Fourth, I believe that a population can be sustained a good deal by the knowledge that really good treatment is available if it is needed, rather in the way that one can derive benefit from the possibility of a medical treatment without actual recourse to it (see Chapter Eight). Just as there are ripples of trauma that radiate a damaging effect, so there are ripples of good care, doing the opposite. In other words, a community that is confident that high quality individualised treatment is happening somewhere in its midst, can avoid the sort of panicked lurching trajectory that causes and perpetuates distress. It can instead accept low-key reassurance, suggestion, advice, and suchlike, delivered by professionals who believe in themselves, believe in their own advice, and only need to deliver it once or twice for it to be taken and acted upon.

Fifth, the integration of mental and physical care, if it is allowed to infiltrate not only at the institutional or organisational level but also at the level of the individual clinician, will enable mental health care (if one must split it off) to be delivered outside of the context of the mental health care service as defined and purchased. That is, all clinicians would be able to respond in a more holistic, mindful, values-based way to symptoms and requests, rather than in an institutionally driven, Cartesian, and reflex way. The same might be true to some extent for teachers, social workers, and, indeed, everyone.

Sixth, placebo, if it could be rescued from the relegation imposed on it by the controlled trial, might turn out to be a relatively inexpensive treatment with little in the way of side effects. I include the placebo effect of services staffed and steered by respected and self-respecting professional clinicians.

Seventh, if the attitude around mental health care and the developmental support of children were to shift towards that of *being with*, most of the people currently employed in the task of telling clinicians what to do and admonishing them for not doing it could instead work as clinicians (teachers, doctors, etc.). They could be trained in the apprenticeship model within a compassionate setting, contributing to the work as they did so, after which they would be welcomed into multidisciplinary teams in which they would continue to develop.

Finally, this is a description of something that I believe should happen between the lines. It is not *the lines themselves*. If I were writing about what mental health provision is needed, I would have a good deal more to say, for example, about prevention. I would want to think about perinatal mental health that involves both parents and wider family, and addresses traumatic and premature births as well as frank mental illness in the mother. I would want a return of the tea-and-toast family centres that I think unobtrusively supported countless struggling parents. I would recommend CAMHS consultation and support to those family centres. I would address at-risk groups, such as looked after children and children receiving general hospital services, not in a prescriptive but in a responsive way using a consultation-liaison approach. I would argue that we should not be trying to save money, but should be spending much more on mental health in particular, and on enabling good entries and exits from life; that human life should be a variable time span characterised by cooperation between us to improve the emotional experience of it, rather than an expensive and fruitless struggle against bad luck, bad judgement, and mortality.

In summary, if a society can support clinical and other services to be wary of materialism and utilitarianism, to shun the politics of fear, and to practise with what I have called therapeutic attitude, then clinical professionals and the society they serve will become healthier.

A TWO-PAGE PRESCRIPTION FOR BEING WITH AND SAYING GOODBYE *IN CHILD AND ADOLESCENT MENTAL HEALTH SERVICES*

For governments, health departments, commissioners , and service managers

1. Create services that provide, for clinicians, the secure base that is necessary for this stressful work.
2. The attitude you hold towards clinicians contributes to the culture in which the patient is treated.
3. Do not be seduced by the notion that risk can be abolished.
4. Understand the potential for "evidence" to alienate humanity.
5. Think about what each of the following says for your own practice.

For clinicians

6. Learn your profession and model of working really well.
7. Try to exercise responsibility for the treatment setting.
8. Develop and practise mindful awareness.
9. Know the value of waiting. Beware automatism.
10. Embrace paradox and learn to sit with uncertainty.
11. Understand and manage your anxiety and that of the system. Do not panic.

12. Enable your patient in his or her development towards individuation, agency, and authenticity.
13. Stand alongside your patient and look at the world together.
14. Be aware of the influence of third party payment.
15. Reawaken faith in the personal.
16. Remember the importance of small things.
17. Learn to discern and work with values and diverse realities.
18. Beware the allure of facts. They can throttle possibility and quench hope.
19. Nurture the creative space between how things are and how they might be.
20. Clinical assessment should not be to apply labels but to establish the need and readiness for, and the likely risks and benefits of, clinical services.
21. Clinical assessment begins a relationship in which there is a duty of care.
22. Nothing quite beats intelligent engagement.
23. Understand that your manner and bearing are treatments.
24. Use iterations of direct observation and qualitative feedback to evaluate and direct treatment in an ongoing way.
25. All behaviours towards and around the patient should be informed at least in part by:
    a. psychodynamic understanding;
    b. behavioural principles;
    c. systemic awareness.
26. Remember the legacies of psychoanalysis.
27. Consider the meaning to your patient of everything you do.
28. Part when it is advisable or unavoidable, and with an eye to the narrative arc.
29. Discuss the ending beforehand. Understand its significance to your patient.
30. Remember possible past and future endings.
31. Make this ending therapeutic.
32. Remember to say goodbye.

REFERENCES

American Psychiatric Association (1994). *Diagnostic and Statistical Manual of Mental Disorders* (4th edn). Washington, DC: American Psychiatric Association.

Baker, R. (2004). Patient-centred care after Shipman. *Journal of the Royal Society of Medicine, 97:* 161–165.

Ballatt, J., & Campling, P. (2011). *Intelligent Kindness: Reforming the Culture of Healthcare.* London: Royal College of Psychiatrists.

Barenboim, D. (2006). *The Reith Lectures: 1. In the Beginning was Sound* [radio programme]. BBC Radio 4. Available at http://www.bbc.co.uk/radio4/features/the-reith-lectures/transcripts/2000/ [accessed 4 April 2015].

Berne, E. (1964). *Games People Play: The Psychology of Human Relationships.* Harmondsworth: Penguin.

Bowlby, J. (1988). *A Secure Base: Clinical Applications of Attachment Theory.* London: Routledge.

Burns, T. (2013). *Our Necessary Shadow: The Nature and Meaning of Psychiatry.* London: Penguin.

Byng-Hall, J. (1995). Creating a secure family base: Some implications of attachment theory for family therapy. *Family Process, 34:* 45–58.

Cardinal, M. (1983). *The Words to Say It* (Trans. P. Goodheart). Cambridge, MA: VanVactor & Goodheart.

Chan, A. -W., & Altman, D. (2005). Identifying outcome reporting bias in randomised trials on PubMed: Review of publications and survey of authors. *British Medical Journal, 330:* 753–756.

Dawkins, R. (1976). *The Selfish Gene.* New York: Oxford University Press.

de Botton, A. (2012). *Religion for Atheists: A Non-believer's Guide to the Uses of Religion.* London: Hamish Hamilton.

Dickinson, E. (1970). In: T. H. Johnson (Ed.), *The Complete Poems of Emily Dickinson.* London: Faber & Faber, 2009.

Dolto, F. (1987). *Tout est langage.* Paris: Vertiges-Carrere [reprinted Paris: Gallimard, 2009].

Dyche, L., & Zayas, L. H. (1995). The value of curiosity and naiveté for the cross-cultural psychotherapist. *Family Process, 34:* 389–399.

Evans, F. J. (1985). Expectancy, therapeutic instructions and the placebo response. In: L. White, B. Tursky, & G. E. Schwarz (Eds.), *Placebo: Theory, Research and Mechanisms* (pp. 215–228). New York: Guilford.

Francis, R. (2013). *Report of the Mid Staffordshire NHS Foundation Trust Public Inquiry: (Volume 2).* London: The Stationery Office.

Fromm, E. (1976). *To Have or To Be?* London: Continuum.

Fulford, K. W. M., Peile, E., & Carroll, H. (2012). *Essential Values-based Practice: Clinical Stories Linking Science with People.* New York: Cambridge University Press.

Gittings, R. (1966). *Selected Poems and Letters of John Keats.* Oxford: Heinemann Educational.

Goldberg, D., & Huxley, P. (1980). *Mental Illness in the Community: The Pathway to Psychiatric Care.* London: Tavistock.

Goldberg, D., Gask, L., & O'Dowd, T. (1989). The treatment of somatization: Teaching techniques of reattribution. *Journal of Psychosomatic Research, 33:* 689–695.

Grossmann, K., Grossmann, K. E., Fremmer-Bombik, E., Kindler, H., Scheurer-Englisch, H., & Zimmermann, P. (2002). The uniqueness of the child-father attachment relationship: Fathers' sensitive and challenging play as a pivotal variable in a 16-year longitudinal study. *Social Development, 11:* 307–331.

Hall, G., Hivernel, F., & Morgan, S. (Eds.) (2009). *Theory and Practice in Child Psychoanalysis: An Introduction to the Work of Françoise Dolto.* London: Karnac.

Hardy, J. N. (2013). Response of the week. *British Medical Journal, 347:* iii. [Full text available in *BMJ Rapid Responses,* 11 September 2013, Communication in difficult situations: What would a friend say? *BMJ, 347:* f5037. Available at http://www.bmj.com/bmj/section-pdf/746284/0 and http://www.bmj.com/content/347/bmj.f5037/rapid-responses, accessed 12 April 2015].

Hayward, J. (Ed.) (1956). *The Penguin Book of English Verse*. London: Penguin [reprinted London: Allen Lane, 1978].

Heidegger, M. (1927). *Sein und Zeit*. Tübingen: Max Niemeyer [Trans. Macquarrie, J., & Robinson, E. (1962). *Being and Time*. Oxford: Blackwell.]

Herriot, P. (2001). *The Employment Relationship: A psychological perspective*. Hove: Routledge.

Holloway, R. (2012). *Leaving Alexandria: A Memoir of Faith and Doubt*. Edinburgh: Canongate, 2013.

Howick, J., Bishop, F. L., Heneghan, C., Wolstenholme, J., Stevens, S., Hobbs, F. D. R., & Lewith, G. (2013). Placebo use in the United Kingdom: Results from a national survey of primary care practitioners. *PLOS One, 8:* E58247. Available at http://journals.plos.org/plosone/article?id=10.1371/journal.pone.0058247 [accessed 6 April 2015].

Hudson, L. (1972). *The Cult of the Fact*. London: Jonathan Cape.

Janis, I. L. (1971). Groupthink. *Psychology Today, 5:* 43–46, 74–76.

Jones, E. (1993). *Family Systems Therapy: Developments in the Milan Systemic Therapies*. Chichester: John Wiley.

Kabat-Zinn, J. (1991). *Full Catastrophe Living: How to Cope with Stress, Pain and Illness Using Mindfulness Meditation*. New York: Dell [reprinted London: Piatkus, 1994].

Kross, E., Berman, M. G., Mischel, W., Smith, E. E., & Wager, T. D. (2011). Social rejection shares somatosensory representations with physical pain. *Proceedings of the National Academy of Sciences of the United States of America, 108:* 6270–6275.

Kundera, M. (1984). *The Unbearable Lightness of Being*. New York: Harper & Row [second edition London: Faber & Faber, 1985].

Lipowski, Z. J. (1967). Review of consultation psychiatry and psychosomatic medicine: 1. General principles. *Psychosomatic Medicine. 29:* 153–171.

Lipowski, Z. J. (1974). Consultation-liaison psychiatry: An overview. *American Journal of Psychiatry, 131:* 623–630.

Lipowski, Z. J. (1986). Somatization: A borderland between medicine and psychiatry. *Canadian Medical Association Journal, 135:* 609–614.

Malan, D. H. (1979). *Individual Psychotherapy and the Science of Psychodynamics*. London: Butterworth.

McGough, R. (1982). *Waving at Trains* . London: Jonathan Cape.

Mears, I. (1922). *Tao Teh King by Lao Tzu: A Tentative Translation from the Chinese*. London: Theosophical Publishing House.

Menzies Lyth, I. (1959). The functions of social systems as a defence against anxiety: A report on a study of the nursing service of a general hospital. *Human Relations, 13:* 95–121 [reprinted in Menzies Lyth, I. (1988). *Containing Anxiety in Institutions: Selected Essays (Volume 1)* (pp. 43–85). London: Free Association].

Metge, J. (1986). *In and Out of Touch: Whakamaa in Cross Cultural Context.* Wellington, NZ: Victoria University Press.

Miller, A. (1987). *The Drama of Being a Child: The Search for the True Self* (Trans. R. Ward). London: Virago.

Mitchell, A. (1982). The apeman who hated snakes. In: *For Beauty Douglas.* London: Allison & Busby.

Mitchell, J. (Ed.) (1986). *The Selected Melanie Klein.* London: Penguin.

National Collaborating Centre for Mental Health (2013). *Psychosis and Schizophrenia in Children and Young People: Recognition and Management: National Clinical Guideline No. 155.* Leicester: The British Psychological Society & London: The Royal College of Psychiatrists.

Ogden, T. H. (2004). On holding and containing, being and dreaming. *International Journal of Psychoanalysis, 85:* 1349–1364.

Onions, C. T. (Ed). (1966). *The Oxford Dictionary of English Etymology.* London: Oxford University Press.

Ougrin, D., Zundel, T., & Ng, A. V. (2009). *Self-harm in Young People: A Therapeutic Assessment Manual.* London: Hodder Arnold.

Park, L. C., & Covi, L. (1965). Nonblind placebo trial: An exploration of neurotic patients' responses to placebo when its inert content is disclosed. *Archives of General Psychiatry, 12:* 336–345.

Pedder, J. R. (1988). Termination reconsidered. *International Journal of Psychoanalysis, 69:* 495–505.

Phillips, A. (1993). On Being Bored. In: *On Kissing, Tickling and Being Bored: Psychoanalytic Essays on the Unexamind Life* (pp. 71–82) London: Faber & Faber, 1994.

Phillips, A. (1994). On Success. In: *On Flirtation.* London: Faber & Faber, 1995.

Pirsig, R. M. (1974). *Zen and the Art of Motorcycle Maintenance: An Inquiry into Values.* London: Bodley Head.

Pullman, P. (1995). *Northern Lights.* London: Scholastic.

Radden, J., & Sadler, J. Z. (2010). *The Virtuous Psychiatrist: Character Ethics in Psychiatric Practice.* New York: Oxford University Press.

Ryle, A., & Kerr, I. B. (2002). *Introducing Cognitive Analytic Therapy: Principles and Practice.* Chichester: John Wiley & Sons.

Saint-Exupéry, A. de (1945). *The Little Prince* (Trans. K. Woods). London: Heinemann.

Salinger, J. D. (1951) *The Catcher in the Rye.* London: Penguin, 1994.

Schulz, K. (2010). *Being Wrong: Adventures in the Margin of Error.* London: Portobello.

Smith, Dame Janet (Chair) (2002–2005). *The Shipman Inquiry: First—Fifth Reports.* Manchester: The Shipman Inquiry.

Spinoza, B. de (1994). *Ethics* (Ed. and Trans. E. Curley). London: Penguin.

Storr, A. (1979). *The Art of Psychotherapy.* London: Secker & Warburg, William Heinemann.

Suzuki, S. (1970). *Zen Mind, Beginner's Mind.* Tokyo: Weatherhill.

Szczeklik, A. (2005). *Catharsis: On the Art of Medicine* (Trans. A. Lloyd-Jones). Chicago, IL: University of Chicago.

Taylor, D. C. (1985). The sick child's predicament. *Australian and New Zealand Journal of Psychiatry, 19*: 130–137.

Thompson, W. G. (2005). *The Placebo Effect and Health: Combining Science and Compassionate Care.* New York: Prometheus.

Watts, A. (1975). *Tao: The Watercourse Way.* Harmondsworth: Penguin.

Watts, A. (1979). *The Wisdom of Insecurity: A Message for an Age of Anxiety.* London: Rider.

Weimer, K., Gulewitsch, M. D., Schlarb, A. A., Schwille-Kiuntke, J., Klosterhalfen, S., & Enck, P. (2013). Placebo effects in children: A review. *Pediatric Research, 74*: 96–102.

White, M., & Epston, D. (1990). *Narrative Means to Therapeutic Ends.* New York: Norton.

Winnicott, D. W. (1957). *The Child and the Outside World.* London: Tavistock.

Winnicott, D. W. (1965). *The Family and Individual Development.* London: Tavistock, 1968.

Winnicott, D. W. (1971a). *Playing and Reality.* Harmondsworth: Penguin, 1974.

Winnicott, D. W. (1971b). *Therapeutic Consultations in Child Psychiatry.* London: Hogarth & The Institute of Psycho-Analysis.

Winnicott, D. W. (1986). Fear of breakdown. In: G. Kohon (Ed.). *The British School of Psychoanalysis: The Independent Tradition* (pp. 173–182). London: Free Association.

Williams, M., Teasdale, J., Segal, Z., & Kabat-Zinn, J. (2007). *The Mindful Way Through Depression.* New York: Guilford.

INDEX